THE
ALTERNATIVE
MEDIA

THE ALTERNATIVE MEDIA

Dismantling Two Centuries of Progress

FRANCIS M. WATSON, JR.

ROCKFORD COLLEGE INSTITUTE

Library of Congress Cataloging in Publication Data

Watson, Francis M.   1921-
    The alternative media, dismantling two centuries of progress.

    Includes bibliographical references and indexes.
    1. Underground press—United States   2. Press and politics—
United States.   I. Title.
PN4888.U5W3   071'.3   79-25916

SINGLE COPIES ARE $5.00. FOR PRICES ON ORDERING LARGE QUANTITIES,
PLEASE CONTACT THE ROCKFORD COLLEGE INSTITUTE, 5050 EAST
STATE STREET, ROCKFORD, ILLINOIS 61101, (815) 226-4016.

THE OPINIONS EXPRESSED IN THE PUBLICATIONS OF THE ROCKFORD
COLLEGE INSTITUTE DO NOT NECESSARILY REFLECT THE POLICIES
OR JUDGMENTS OF ROCKFORD COLLEGE.

CONTENTS

The Embattled Leadership
An Introductory Comment

This is not a good era for leaders. Chroniclers of the contemporary scene note that in all fields of endeavor there is a scarcity of individuals who are nationally acclaimed and respected. The implication seems to be that the American bloodline has run out of the stuff of greatness. What has actually happened is that there is no longer a consensus as to what is forward motion and what is backward, so that anyone who is successful in moving the group in any direction is subject to criticism from within the ranks of his own organization as well as from professional commentators. Acclaim from some quarters is balanced with censure from others.

The person now serving in a position of leadership is like a coach trying to guide a team in a game wherein players on both sides disregard the rules with impunity and the spectators are at liberty to attack if they are so inclined. The concepts which used to provide the rules for the public life of the citizen are in disarray. Industriousness, thrift, loyalty, self-reliance, lawfulness, patriotism, truthfulness, morality, idealism, fairness, integrity, altruism and piety have all, like the currency, been devalued. *In a free nation, the economic consequences of abandoning the gold standard are as nothing compared to the cultural convulsions that occur when the virtue standard is discarded.*

Undisciplined conduct and unpredictable public reactions bewilder and cripple all the institutions of society. There is as much confusion in the family council as in the corporate board room. Churches, legislative bodies, the professions, the banks, the armed services, the courts, the colleges and the social service agencies are equally uncertain about how to fulfill their respective purposes and still deal with the torrent of challenge and abuse and the governmental interference that has been generated by the critics.

There are no precedents to point the way for a people that no longer accepts any definitions of right and wrong. Each corrective action must spawn new difficulties when every group is vulnerable to

1

attack by those who seek profit for themselves in pressing a grievance they have discovered or invented, assured that the go-for-the-jugular press will reinforce the attack. *Just as living organisms can survive only in appropriate environmental conditions, their vital functions affected by temperature, moisture, chemicals, gases, etc., so the vital functions of social institutions are dependent upon the cultural climate in which they operate.* Perhaps the time has arrived when cultural pollution can be recognized as a lethal agent, sapping the vitality of all organized activity.

This study of the alternative press examines one of the principal wellsprings of cultural pestilence. The designation, *alternative* press, reflects the common denominator of a host of otherwise disparate publications, all of them committed to the radical alteration or elimination of the traditional American institutions. Thus malevolent—ill-wishing—is a precise description of this sector of the press.

The import of this study is threefold:

1. Many people are only dimly aware of the existence and the scope of the alternative press;

2. The so-called *establishment* press, which claims to reflect American opinion and is generally presumed to defend the established American institutions, has consistently publicized and often eventually advocated the views and the campaigns proposed by the *alternative* press; and

3. The individuals, organizations or industries upon whom the *alternatives* are to be imposed (the U.S. defense system, the nuclear energy industry, etc.) are usually unaware that they are the chosen targets of the alternative press or that the campaign has even been launched until it has gathered a good head of steam.

In preparing and presenting this analysis, it is our hope that it may be useful to those charged with responsibilities for the success of private enterprise and the other institutions of a free society.

JOHN A. HOWARD
DIRECTOR
ROCKFORD COLLEGE INSTITUTE

ONE

The Background

The recent forebears of the alternative press were a small group of avant-garde publications that appeared in the mid-1950s, among them the *Village Voice* and the *Realist*, both of New York City, and the *Berkeley Barb*, Berkeley, California. In language, cartoons, pictures and subject matter, they pioneered the frontal assault upon the dominant taboos and traditions of the land. They served as a training ground for editors and writers who helped to launch the publications in the self-designated category of "the underground press."

The Origins of the Alternative Press

The real surge of underground papers did not come until a decade after the *Village Voice* hit the streets of Greenwich Village in 1955. The "undergrounds" began to multiply when the fervor and experience generated in the civil rights movement were redirected to issues brought into prominence by Mario Savio and his cohorts in their confrontation with the University of California at Berkeley.

Taking their cue from the printed materials that had proliferated in the metropolitan "hippie" communes, activist-prone college students, drop-outs and hangers-on began to produce their own tracts, pamphlets and tabloids designed for a campus clientele. The causes were many: The ongoing concern for civil rights, sexual liberation, "filthy speech," agitation against the Vietnam War, psychedelic drugs, draft evasion, and the elimination of campus parietal rules constituted a heady brew, proclaimed with indignant righteousness under the banners of social justice and freedom. Other issues were soon added: the demand for student determination of the academic program, the insistence that military research not be tolerated in the academy, the call for the elimination of ROTC, the hue and cry against the military-industrial complex, and the barring of the campus to corporate and military recruiting officers.

As these cause-oriented papers broadened the range of issues to be covered and increased the intensity of their attacks on the institutions and practices of the society, they also broadened their audiences. They reached out into the high schools and penetrated military bases, both in the U.S. and overseas. There evolved an editorial amalgam of cultural rebellion and radical politics. The underground press was born—and it caught on. It spread from California and New York into other states on the West Coast and in New England, into the Midwest, down the East Coast, and into the South. The number of papers published throughout the country jumped from a mere handful in 1964 and 1965 to more than 300 by 1968, over 400 in 1969, at least 500 by early 1970, and to probably more than 800, in some 40 states, by late 1971.

At first one could find a certain spontaneity in the papers popping up here and there across the country. Many exhibited a high degree of individual creativity. They were hailed by their defenders, mainly in academia, as the "new journalism" or, even then, as "alternative papers," and sometimes as the "journalism of dissent." They were praised as outlets for the newly found "social awareness" of the youth.

This "awareness" soon turned to bitterness. Laurence Leamer, the young *Newsweek* writer who traveled about the country visiting with and interviewing members of the staffs of underground papers, wrote that when "they looked for new tools to end racism in America and bring the GIs home from Vietnam, they were drawn inexorably not toward a revitalized cultural radicalism but to Marxism and political revolution. These ideas could not help but affect the underground press, and by 1971 there were many papers that thought of themselves as propaganda weapons in the struggle for worldwide Marxist revolution."[1]

Many of these papers moved deeper and deeper into the politics of the far left, justifying this transition by claiming complete frustration in trying to "work within the system." Increasingly, they identified with Che Guevara, Castro, Mao Tse-tung, Lenin and Trotsky.

Although the name "underground" papers had been in use for some time, that designation took on a fuller meaning. Identifying themselves with the World War II underground papers in fighting against fascism and Nazism, a number of papers began to call America a "fascist state" and spelled it Ameri*k*a, sometimes working a swastika into the *k*. They proclaimed their kinship with modern rebels and revolutionaries around the globe—German and Italian terrorist groups, Irish rebels, Palestinians, various African organizations, "people's armies" in Argentina and Brazil, the Tupamaro guerrillas in Uruguay, and the National Liberation Front in Vietnam. They published countless suggestions about the tactics and weaponry for carrying out the "revolution" in the United States.

They also cooperated in the development of an "underground railroad" on the model of the Civil War conduit for escaped slaves. As opposition to the Vietnam War became more intense, draft resistance became a major cause for the underground press. Draft evaders were sheltered and assisted in their clandestine movements about the United States, to Canada and even to Sweden.

As acts of terrorism multiplied—bombings, arson, sabotage, sniping and political kidnapping—the underground network was put to use to move people, weapons and explosives and to protect the perpetrators from apprehension by the police and the FBI. These criminal activities had the fervent support of the underground press and sometimes included the direct involvement of underground editors and journalists. Most Americans were only dimly aware of the underground newspapers, but for the young people engaged in the street and campus actions, the papers served as handbooks, directories, a communications network, and provided a sense of national camaraderie and mutual encouragement.

In order to advance the cause of political radicalism, the underground press sought to alienate the nation's youth from the values and traditions of their society. By encouraging defiance of the draft laws, by promoting the use of illegal drugs, by the regular use of gutter language and by trumpeting the joys of sexual promiscuity, all the while insisting on the "right" to do these things, they induced a great many college students to take up practices that would create a gulf between them and the adult society. When parents, college officers and clergymen tried to counsel against these activities, there was a tendency among the young to feel misunderstood and persecuted, a state of mind that lends itself to radicalization. As their radicalism gathered momentum, the underground papers began to publish strategies for subverting or overthrowing existing institutions, and outlined the tactics for guerrilla warfare and gave instructions for the use of weapons and the making of crude bombs. They reported extensively on the activities of revolutionary organizations both at home and abroad. For example, they reprinted material received from guerrilla movements in Latin America, the Middle East, Africa and from the Viet Cong and the North Vietnamese government. They cheered the Weathermen for detonating bombs in New York and Washington, robbing a bank in Massachusetts and engineering a jailbreak in California. The underground press was the prime agency for enlisting the crowds which came from all over the country to disrupt the Democratic National Convention in Chicago.

In 1968 Ethel Romm, writing in the magazine, *New York*, predicted that the then two or three hundred underground papers could have this country "twitching from one coast to the other . . . they put it all down in writing and nobody reads it . . . the freak show distracts the public from the main event." The main event was the undermining of the traditional institutions, values, relationships and patterns of conduct of the society. The underground papers were kindling, stoking and fanning the fires of the counterculture. The government, the church, national foreign policy, the family, the educational system—all were castigated and ridiculed relentlessly. And from the beginning, the business community was the primary target for attack.

Underground Papers and the Business Community

It is ironic that business organizations were instrumental in the initiation and growth of the underground press, since their advertising revenues sometimes provided the financial margin for their survival. When a paper began, its commercial advertising was usually restricted to a few entertainment and clothing ads from local businesses. The more militant papers were philosophically selective in the ads they would carry, rejecting corporate promotional materials except those related to rock music. From the early days, however, there were some willing papers with an extensive readership that were chosen as corporate advertising vehicles. As far back as 1969, *Business Week* reported that advertisers, having discovered the underground papers as a sure-fire means for reaching the youth market, were channeling extensive advertising funds into these outlets, despite their militant antibusiness biases.

Long before a pattern of antibusiness sentiment began to surface in the "Establishment" press, it was standard fare in the underground papers. From the beginning, business and industrial corporations were the subject of vicious cartoons, hostile mock advertising, and a steady chorus charging private enterprise with "enslaving the employees and robbing the consumers." Thus, Ralph Nader developed an instant following on the campuses as soon as he became known.

In 1970 (the year Ralph Nader's associate launched the "Campaign to Make G. M. Responsible"), a national sampling of the underground press revealed that the most common antibusiness themes and the ones receiving the most space were (in order of rank): 1) the big corporation seen as a monster—often with monster or bloated "Wall Street investor" cartoons in accompaniment; 2) the automobile industry; 3) telephone companies; 4) oil companies; 5) home furnishings and appliances; 6) synthetic manufacturers; 7) the food industry; 8) banks; 9) the soft-drink industry.

In conjunction with this categorized hostility, these papers sometimes provided detailed instructions for shoplifting, making long
distance calls without paying, or charging calls to a corporate credit
card, getting into theaters and other places of entertainment without
paying, punching extra holes in machine-produced bills "so the
computers will freak out," or instructions for sabotaging computer
equipment. (Such "tips" still appear in some of the alternative press.)
The rationale for these campaigns usually included the assertion that
it is not really stealing to take anything from a business because all
businesses steal from the people constantly and when you take from
them, you are only taking what belongs to "the people" already.

In another dimension of its anticapitalism, the underground press
regularly sided with labor in its disputes with management, publicizing
the workers' complaints and providing favorable stories about the
labor leaders. Sometimes the papers themselves would assume the role
of agitators in boycotts of local businesses they charged with unfair
labor or merchandising practices.

The development of countercultural papers was encouraged,
assisted and guided by the Underground Press Syndicate. This New
York operation was founded in 1966 by a small group of underground
editors and activists who frequented the office of the drug-culture
paper, *East Village Other.* Tom Forcade, who later founded a slick-
paper magazine for drug users, called *High Times,* was the Underground
Press Syndicate's first full-time coordinator. Through the distribution
to its member editors of copies of other papers from across the country,
it contributed to a national homogenization of the causes to be urged
and the mottoes and phraseology for their advocacy. Thus dramatic
commentary or arresting visual material appeared again and again,
often modified to fit the local scene of a paper far distant from the point
of origin. A striking photograph of a placard carrier, or a picket with
upraised fist caught by an underground newspaper camera in Atlanta
might appear a couple of weeks later in a paper in Massachusetts or
Washington State, several weeks later in Michigan and even months
later in Texas. Texts and drawings, including some of the previously
mentioned "tips" on how to "rip off" businesses, were reprinted nationwide, sometimes with local attributions or connections and sometimes
accurately citing the originating paper. Some items, passed from paper
to paper, eventually led to syndication in the true sense. This was
especially true of comic strip sequences. One example was an eleven-
panel cartoon strip that appeared in papers in every section of the
country, entitled "the amazing pedestrian mind takes on the avaricious
pig capitalist." It portrayed the capitalist castigating a captive scientist
because he had not produced a "money-making invention all week!"
The scientist finally produces a grotesque-looking creature that
resembles a brain with legs—the "pedestrian mind"—which, in obvious

glee, eats both the scientist and the capitalist. To the initiates, this was quickly recognized as a reminder of Karl Marx's contention: "Capitalism bears the seeds of its own destruction."

As the papers began to focus on particular industries and corporations, the automobile industry was an early target, expectedly agitated about "pollution" but equally solicitous about labor relations. Most of the papers used allegations of the industry's mistreatment of its employees as a springboard for promoting alliances between members of the "working class" and the activists in the underground press movement. The Students for a Democratic Society had called for "student-worker" alliances and a number of papers sent staff members into industrial communities "to learn how the people live, gain their confidence, and 'talk politics' with them." The papers also supported invitations for militant or patently radical workers to be invited to speak on campuses and were generous in their coverage of the grievances alleged by such speakers.

The Vietnam War became the most frequent topic among the underground papers and during the height of that conflict it received their continuous attention. Usually, the war turned out to be only a point of departure for attacking other "evils" of the society. A favorite theme was the "imperialism" of large corporations and their stake in continuing the war "in order to sell war material and protect their interests in Southeast Asia." The automobile and oil industries were favorite targets of alternative journalistic venom and, in time, all multinational corporations were on their "hit" parade.

The 'Death' of the Underground Press

Eventually the market was sated with the unbridled rhetoric of revolution and violence. In 1972 and 1973 many of the papers that had been published for several years were terminated—the *Berkeley Tribe*, New York's *Rat*, the *Chicago Seed*, Boston's *Old Mole*, and the *San Francisco Good Times* among them.[2] Many did not die off, but took on a more civilized veneer and continued working toward the same goals but labeling themselves "alternative" newspapers. The *Free Venice Beachhead*, the *Straight Creek Journal*, the *Boston Phoenix*, the *Real Paper*, Wisconsin's *Take Over* and the *Bugle American* in Wisconsin, and the *North Carolina Anvil* are examples. Those that did die were generally replaced by one or more alternative papers in the same locality. But the new designation of "alternative press" did not signal any fundamental change. An "anti-Establishment" heart still pumped the blood.

The change to a new image was anticipated as early as 1968 when Tom Forcade, the "coordinator" of the Underground Press Syndicate, wrote in his own magazine:

> " 'Underground' is a sloppy word and a lot of us are sorry we got stuck with it. 'Underground' is meaningless, ambiguous, irrelevant, wildly imprecise, undefinitive, derivative..."[3]

Eventually the name of his organization began to appear as the Alternative Press Syndicate, without changing a digit in its post office box number or anything else about its operation. The same transition gradually took place among the individual papers.

Whether Tom Forcade was serious or merely romping in his remarks about the term "underground," it is clear that there were two substantive reasons for discarding that title. One was cosmetic. The other was strategic. After an intense interfactional debate that lasted several years, there was a fundamental shift among "New Leftists" from a violent to a nonviolent strategy for remaking the society into some form of socialism. A street language version of what this really meant in the inner circles of "the movement" is offered by the following exchange, in late 1969, between a radical radio newsman and a practitioner of the violent strategy. The young man being interviewed—speaking from intricately arranged anonymity—claimed to be a member of the Weatherman organization, and to have been involved in bombings in the San Francisco area:

> "QUESTION: You speak of the revolution in this country coming together under the umbrella of communism. It would seem, at least for now, that communism has a very small following here.
>
> ANSWER: I think that the following that communism—let's call it the movement for socialism—has in America is bigger than most people imagine. When people opt for socialism, it's not necessarily on the basis of having the book-understanding of what socialism means. People move for socialism on the basis of what the [expletive] is empirically necessary."[4]

This is a succinct statement of the philosophy obtaining among the extremists who were at the core of the underground press. Whether they all agreed on the eventual goal this young Weatherman described or not, their papers did not refute it. The ceaseless argument was over *strategy,* not goals. The change in strategy was dictated ultimately by what happened to the Students for a Democratic Society (SDS). Essentially the SDS *was* the "New Left" in the late 1960s, and it was the most powerful single influence in the development and proliferation of underground papers.

SDS's plan for changing the society had increasingly become a bone of contention, with some members insisting upon violence, or

"Revolution Now!" and others equally determined to follow a nonviolent course, "going out to organize among the communities and in the work places" of the larger society. The incredibly long and complex deliberation over these strategic choices came to a head in the 1969 SDS national convention in Chicago. It was an amazing affair, indeed. Although it was a conference of self-styled idealists who clamored for "openness" and "participatory democracy," it was closed to the public and the press. In his book, *SDS*, Kirkpatrick Sale wrote of that meeting:

> "Slowly the delegates filed into the mammoth Coliseum...Around the edges of the hall the various sects and groupuscles had set up tables to display their ideological wares and entice unwary delegates: Progressive Labor, the International Socialists, the Young Socialist Alliance, Communists, Spartacists, Wobblies, anarchists, Yippies, and assorted others. Adding to the paper barrage were pamphlets and mimeographed sheets from every tendency within SDS: The RYM [Revolutionary Youth Movement] people came with a series of exposés of PL's [Progressive Labor's] dangerous behavior, PL provided documents reaffirming its correctness, REP [Radical Education Project] arrived with neat booklets setting out the RYM position and how it had worked in the past six months, the Bay Area Radical Union [from whence came the Revolutionary Union/Revolutionary Communist Party] presented its 'Red Papers' putting forth a pro-Maoist but anti-PL version of militant revolution, and New York anarchists offered Murray Bookchin's sprightly 'Listen, Marxist' denouncing *all* of the other SDS tendencies. And to each of the delegates was handed the convention issue of *New Left Notes* [the official SDS newspaper], full of proposals and amendments, in which the pride of place went to an extraordinary article covering six solid pages with dense type (the longest article the paper had ever run), decorated with pictures of Marx, Lenin, Mao, and a recurring silhouette of armed guerrillas growing larger from first page to last. The title of the piece, cryptic for many, was, 'You Don't Need a Weatherman to Know Which Way the Wind Blows.' [This last, of course, was the manifesto from which the Weatherman organization was formed.]"[5]

There ensued two days of fiery speeches, power struggles, microphone grabs and walkouts which ended with the organization in such a shambles that it soon ceased to exist as a national entity. When it was over, the nuclei of several new organizations had splintered off, and two or three older organizations had seized upon some of the SDS's chapter assets. No viable leadership was left in the center. Those who had seemed to be the most promising of the national officers, women and men, opted for violence. Putting their ideas into action, they walked out, taking with them the physical assets of the national headquarters, records, lists and money, and founded the Weatherman organization. Subsequently, they made a trip to Cuba, issued a number of fire-breathing statements, sent out recruiting teams, held a dramatically proclaimed "war council," and went "underground." They proceeded over the next several years to set off some bombs in public buildings in various parts of the country, to issue defiant "communiqués" about "the revolution," and to fascinate the readers of underground newspapers with accounts of both. In the early months of their rampage, they managed to get three of their members killed when a "bomb factory" they were operating in an expensive Manhattan townhouse accidentally exploded, but their subsequent success with hit-and-run tactics, while eluding the police of several cities and the FBI for years, gave real meaning to the word "underground."

Meanwhile, the argument over strategy continued month after month, sometimes filling pages in the underground papers, until it came to its second, though less flamboyant, head in a general discrediting of the Weathermen's "adventurism." While they remained as superstars of "the struggle," and darted out periodically to prove themselves as such, the debate was won by the advocates of the "nonviolent" route. And the strategy shift gradually spread throughout most of the amorphous radical fermentation that had come to be called "the movement."

Undergrounds Become Alternatives

By the summer of 1973, although the Weathermen, the fringes of which were to figure in the Symbionese Liberation Army's escapades following the Hearst kidnapping, were still ranging about the country, nonviolence had won out with the radical newspapers. In June of 1973 a meeting was held in Boulder, Colorado. By that time, almost all of the surviving papers were in financial trouble, and many had died in the preceding eighteen months. Representatives of fifty of the stalwarts came together to try to work out some of their problems. One report of this gathering read:

> "The attending papers varied greatly: Their politics, organizational structure, and funding being as various as their names. The main tie amongst these papers was some identification with the political Left, financial instability, and a stubborn determination to communicate information which would not otherwise be available."[6]

The deliberations were reported to have included politics and methods of coordinating the publications staff, but the primary focus seems to have been "practical matters (distribution, advertising)." Here emerges the "cosmetic" reason for the switch to the "alternative" label; it promised to be more palatable to distributors, advertisers and financial backers.

They did not have to invent the term. They had been using it all along, to refer to the institutions and lifestyles they had been promoting in their pages from the beginning—alternative education, schools and universities; alternative families, child-care systems, and marriages; alternative economics, collectivist enterprises and communal farming; alternative politics, socialist systems and anarchist propositions; and, indeed, an alternative society. There had been a number of publications in the underground press that had incorporated the word "alternative" in their titles, such as *Alternatives Magazine,* a running directory and news source on communes; *Alternate Society,* a pulp-paper magazine dealing primarily with collectivist economic ideas; and Alternatives Features Services, a source of countercultural feature material for underground papers. There were organizations as well as publications then, and more now, using "alternative" in their names—in the 1960s: Alternatives Foundation, Alternative Enterprise Exchange, and Alternatives for Peace; and now in the late 1970s: Alternative Energy Coalition, Alternative Vocations, and Alternative State and Local Public Policies, among others.

Perhaps the earliest of these was the Alternatives Foundation. It dated from at least 1966 when it began publishing a magazine called *Modern Utopian.* Its editor reported the magazine's editorial policies to include: favoring legalization of abortion, marijuana and psychedelic drugs; the establishment and growth of "experimental communities" or communes of various types; sexual freedom; the ending of poverty through a guaranteed annual income; the "secularization and reform of orthodox religions"; free schools, that is, nonstructured education; and the elimination of racism.[7]

A recently formed organization with the potential for profound impact on the society is the National Conference on Alternative State and Local Public Policies.[8] Its literature describes it as a "nationwide network of public officials, community organizers, trade union leaders, and public policy experts who represent what might be called the Programmatic Left." In other words, it is aimed at installing leftist policies and programs in state and local governments through the efforts of minority members of those governments who consult with each other in the course of their efforts. The *Washington Post* (July 17, 1978) described it as a vehicle for continued communication and cooperation among "some of the more prominent young radical political activists of the 1960s" who are now scattered in government at the state and local levels. In other words, alternative public policies are really those devised by *young radical political activists*—i. e., the "New Left" of a few years ago. The "New Left," it seems, differs from the "Old Left" primarily in its refusal to be apologists for the Soviet Union. It says, in effect, "The USSR is not a good example of what we have in mind. The doctrine of Marxist-Leninism is still valid, but the Soviet leaders have misapplied and perverted it."

The National Conference on Alternative State and Local Public Policies, headed by a former bureau chief of the avowed Marxist-Leninist newspaper, the *Guardian,* is a subsidiary of the Institute for Policy Studies (IPS), itself a composite of *radical political activists* whose ideological orientation apparently ranges from "Democratic Left" to Trotskyite and Chilean/Cuban communism. The IPS is committed to "working within the system" at the national level, and provides analyses and working papers to sympathetic members of Congress. The IPS and its subsidiary, which operates at the state and local levels, provide a powerful mechanism for persuading American government to move leftward by small legislative and executive increments. Somewhere in this, one may hear an echo of the words of the young Weathermen being interviewed by the radical radio newsman: "When people [in the U. S.] opt for socialism, it's not necessarily on the basis of having the book-understanding of what socialism means."

And this is finally what the term "alternative politics" means to those who are promoting it. It does not mean simply proposing an option for public consideration. It means the rejection of the present system in favor of a radically different one. In other words, whatever the dictionary may tell us about the meaning of "alternative," its replacement of "underground" is clearly intended as the rhetoric of deception.

TWO

Alliances
and
Maturity

The Alternative Press Comes of Age

"The alternative press is now respectable enough to be edgy about being called alternative. Apparently, the word was actually an attempt at respectability in the first place—a way for proprietors of certain weeklies to distinguish their papers from the underground press—but when it is uttered out loud inside of a bank or an advertising agency, it still seems to give off little puffs of incense and marijuana smoke. Representatives of about thirty alternative weeklies met recently in Seattle to discuss, among other matters, the possibility of forming a sort of trade association . . ."[9]

"They have their spiritual roots, most of them, in the 1960s—in the self-styled 'underground' newspapers that were as stridently opposed to the Vietnam War, the police and every manifestation of the corporate Establishment as they were dedicated to racial equality, sexual freedom, campus reform and mind-expanding drugs . . ."[10]

The two articles excerpted above were reporting on a four-day meeting of editors and publishers of thirty "alternative weeklies" in Seattle during February of 1978. The main concerns of the meeting seem to have been the economic ways and means of pursuing a brand of journalism described frankly, but not critically, in the *Los Angeles Times* article as "anti-Establishment and generally to the left of the political center."

There were long and lively exchanges of ideas during the four days and there was an undercurrent of disagreement about whether economics or ideology should have primacy in alternative journalism. Apparently the *Los Angeles Times* article was accurate in its description of the common philosophical bent of these journalists. There was no argument on the product design, only on how well it should be made to pay.

As the *Times* article pointed out, some of the participants in the conference were obviously involved in alternative journalism solely because of their "strong ideological commitments," but others were quite as obviously involved to attain economic success. Indeed, the pure ideologues, usually from papers with a circulation from two to five thousand and a bare subsistence level of revenue, were distressed that their colleagues did not seem to share their commitment. They claimed they would feel guilty about making a profit from their publishing ventures. In the opposing group were papers with circulations in the tens of thousands and annual revenues in the hundreds of thousands, or even millions, of dollars.

Both reports of the Seattle meeting end with a sort of "And that's that," as if the differences between the two factions had been accommodated and that was the major point of interest for the public. Nothing could be further from the truth. The alternative, alias underground, press exerts an exceedingly powerful influence in the American culture and economy, an influence which has had a far greater impact through the last fifteen years than most people understand. Reports that the radical thrust has abated grossly mislead the public and even stir some sparks among the radicals.

The *Los Angeles Times'* account of the Seattle conference, having noted that the meeting coincided with Bella Abzug's failure in her bid to return to Congress and Leon Spinks' victory over Muhammad Ali, commented, "In a sense it was the week that the 1960s were formally and finally interred." The common assumption that "all of that" is behind us prompted an outburst that appeared in the *Washington Post* in July of 1978. The credit statement reads: "The writer is a poet. This article is adapted from one in the *Free Venice Beachhead*, an alternative newspaper published by a Venice (Cal.) collective."

This alternative paper had made its transition from "underground" to "alternative" without altering anything in its character. The item published by the *Post* read:

> "I'm tired of reading about the 'demise of the counterculture.' It's one of the mass media's favorite subjects, and it's become a boring cliché.

> The fact is, the people who are so determined to prove that a counterculture no longer exists—or that the turbulent era of the '60s has had no lasting effect on America—are downright wrong.

> Watch closely the next time a TV newsman eulogizes the '60s. Chances are, his hair is longer than John Lennon's was in 1964. Even professional athletes are unabashedly growing beards and have their hair permed.

> Of course, the effects of social change go deeper than hair, facial or otherwise. For instance, at the start of the '60s, almost all of us

15

expected to get married and have children. Nowadays, some couples choose simply to live together. Many married couples do not have children; some couples have children without being married. Then there are openly homosexual couples, some of whom live with children of one or the other member of the partnership; individuals who simply prefer to live alone, and those who form communes. All these alternatives are increasingly more 'acceptable' today than they were 10 years ago.

Education has changed, too. Everyone says that colleges are 'going back to the basics,' but extension programs, off-beat lecture series, seminars, workshops and ethnic studies are all here to stay—or seemed to be, before Proposition 13. And don't forget coed dorms, unheard of in the early 1960s.

Moreover, a number of states have partly decriminalized marijuana use, and more drug-law reforms appear to be on the way. And, although a great deal remains to be done, noticeable milestones have been passed on the road to achieving full civil rights for all Americans.

Perhaps most important of all, the 1960s legacy of nonconformity and experimentation has left the country subtly and positively different. The 1970s have not been without change either. To say that there has been no radical activity in this decade is to negate the feminist movement, the gay movement, the native American movement, the antinuke movement . . ."[11]

The article could have cited many other movements: The antifamily movement, the antisports movement, the antibusiness movement, the antimilitary movement, and the anti-intelligence movement. It could have listed the consumerist movement, the affirmative action movement, the sex education movement, the regulatory movement, the "corporate responsibility" movement, the radical education and radical religion movements, and the movements to support guerrilla activities in other countries. It could also have added the welfare rights movement, the public health care movement, and the child care movement. *Every one of these was actively and militantly promoted* by the underground press a few years ago, and today is being advocated just as vigorously and more widely under the laundered label of the alternative press.

The articles cited at the beginning of this section suggest that most of the "alternative weeklies" at the Seattle conference had their "spiritual roots" in the underground newspapers. As a matter of fact, half of the papers they cite by name *are* former underground papers.[12] Half of those, in turn, are still listed as members of the Alternative Press Syndicate.[13]

The *Los Angeles Times* identified alternative weeklies as "anti-Establishment and left of political center," with a circulation of from two to a hundred thousand, and with some easily discernible ties to the concept of underground or alternative journalism. It estimated that there are about fifty such publications. Actually, the total is probably over a hundred. If the criteria are extended to include biweekly and quarterly publications and newsletters and magazine formats, the number must be in excess of a thousand. Expanded to include the electronic media and the film makers with discernible ties to the underground or alternative media, the total is probably more than 1,200. The literature of the Alternative Press Syndicate states that there are alternative publications in "most American cities." Our analysis shows alternative weeklies in 34 of the 50 largest cities in the country, in addition to 49 cities not among the 50 largest. Under the expanded criteria cited above, we have identified some type of underground/alternative publication in all but four of the 50 largest cities.[14]

Four Powerful Allies of the Alternative Press

Turning to the nature and impact of the individual publications, we begin with two that seldom appear in listings of alternative papers, the *Guardian* and the *Militant*. Both have solid credentials in the developmental history of the underground/alternative press, and both have a national circulation of about 20,000. From the standpoint of the quality of phraseology and readability, the *Guardian* is among the most impressive tabloids in the country. It comes from a long liberal tradition. It was founded by Henry Wallace's Progressive Party in 1948, as the *National Guardian*, and was subsequently taken over by "New Leftists" in the late 1960s. It is candid about its "anti-Establishment" policies and specific about the flavor of its leftism, frankly advocating the displacement of the system with communism on the Chinese model. The *Militant* is equally open about its objective—communism of a Trotskyite nature. It is the organ of the U. S. Socialist Workers Party. Like the *Guardian,* the *Militant* has been circulating among "New Leftists" for more than a decade and has been in the thick of the underground/alternative journalism from the beginning.

In both cases, the political partisanship is too blatant for acceptance into the various associations of alternative weeklies. In order to qualify, a publication must be "able to pass"—that is, give the impression that it is seeking justice within the conceptual framework of the free society.

Two other important publications that are excluded from the alternative category are the *Berkeley Barb* and Madison, Wisconsin's *Take Over.* Both have underground and alternative credentials and both have reputations for vigorous muckraking, a prized designation among alternative papers. But both the *Barb* and *Take Over* have always aimed for a narrowly radical audience, and they look it. They call them-selves community papers but the boundaries of community as they see it have nothing to do with geography, or even age group. They aim for people interested in far-out radical activism. Three years ago *Take Over* ran what some people read as a sick-humor spread on kidnapping — including the names and addresses of forty executives of large corpor-ations, along with a figure each corporation was judged capable of paying for the ransom of its chief executive. Such antics do not make *Take Over* welcome in affiliated "newsweekly" circles.

Two publications that the *Los Angeles Times* story mentioned but claimed "cannot rightly be regarded as either 'underground' or 'alter-native' newspapers" were the New York *Village Voice* and the nation-ally circulated *Rolling Stone.* Technically there is merit to this claim; functionally there is really none. Neither publication ever grubbed around in the streets or wrestled in the mob scenes of the campuses, as most of the full-fledged undergrounds did. Yet, both probably had more to do with the promulgation of the cultural and political ideas of the underground newspapers than did any of the "undergrounds."

Of the *Village Voice* the British underground newspaper editor, Richard Neville, wrote in his book, *Play Power: Exploring the Inter-national Underground:*

"The contemporary explosion of antisociety, *mass circulation* news-papers and magazines was detonated, if belatedly, by the success of the Greenwich Village newspaper, the *Village Voice* . . . first published in October, 1955 . . . showed that a newspaper could be run by amateurs, and that a relatively permissive editorial policy did not necessarily mean commercial suicide. The *Voice* is now the grand old man of the Underground, often shocked by its own progeny. Its columns acknowledge the existence of the new breed of publications, but its advertising manager is disinclined to accept their revenue."[15]

Speaking more directly to the mechanics of how the *Village Voice* begat its progeny, the American college professor, Robert Glessing, wrote in his book, *The Underground Press in America*, that:

". . . the *Voice* was the first newspaper in the history of modern American journalism to consistently report news with no restriction on language, a policy widely adopted by underground editors to shock the authority structure."[16]

In other words, the *Village Voice* assaulted the society's taboo against the use of what were called "four-letter words" in a newspaper. It did so, however, in the midst of a Greenwich Village avant-garde that was notorious for its Bohemianism, and little notice was taken of the matter elsewhere. The underground papers copied the practice a decade later and used it as a bludgeon against the sensitivities of "Middle America." They put these forbidden words in large, bold letters on the front pages of tabloids that were passed out in the streets, on college campuses, and on public school grounds. This alone would have been a considerable jolt to the "middle-class ethic." Indeed, various obscenity-impact studies to the contrary notwithstanding, militants recruiting foot troops for rioting in the streets quickly noted that if you can get a nice middle-class girl to use language like that, and to scream such words out loud at a rally, you have a much better chance of getting her to throw a brick through a plate glass window!

Of course, the *Village Voice* had never given much attention to the niceties of throwing bricks through windows or making bombs or any of the other means of violence that were common to the pages of the underground papers. In fact, from all appearances, Richard Neville was correct — it has often been "shocked by its own progeny." Indeed, it is unlikely that the *Village Voice* was interested in the use of obscenities as weapons of political radicalization. Rather, it appeared to be interested merely in loosening up the culture, in promoting its avant-garde perspective of the arts, literature, films and entertainment, and celebrating the "do your own thing" philosophy. It has used four-letter words only to be more explicit and sensual. Its purpose was to influence the culture toward greater permissiveness.

Indeed, the founders of the *Village Voice*, Jerry Tollmer, Norman Mailer, Edwin Fancher, Daniel Wolf and John Wilcock, were not notably political in their orientation. And the periodical they originated is still not extensively involved in politics. Yet its contents, nearly 200 pages of them week in and week out, illustrate how permissive culture translates into permissive politics. By the sheer volume of the material in its pages, the *Village Voice* provides a force for self-indulgence in art and lifestyle that runs counter to the values of self-discipline and economic self-reliance associated with capitalism and liberty. When homosexuality or the public funding of abortions are at issue in political contests, the *Village Voice* is likely to support the liberal candidate and oppose the other on cultural rather than political grounds. In economic matters, the *Village Voice* is by and large hostile to business and distrustful of capitalism.

So, too, is *Rolling Stone*. This tabloid, looking upon itself as a magazine and not a newspaper, is only about half the size of the *Village Voice*, but is also ad-fat, and has a very large national circulation which includes young adults as well as teen-agers, with extensive sales from news counters across the country.

Whereas the *Village Voice* preceded the underground papers, and some of its staff actually gave them a helping hand, the *Rolling Stone* grew out of this environment but has held itself aloof from its peers. It behaved and looked different from the majority of underground papers from the beginning. It did not involve itself in the fray in the streets, but that was by no means the only difference. It was founded by an individual who obviously intended to make money with it, with no apparent concern about the impact of its editorial policy upon "the system." And it has made money, enough so that it could afford to lose a reported million dollars trying to start a second publication, *Outside.*

As in the case of the *Village Voice,* most of *Rolling Stone's* space is, and always has been, taken up with cultural rather than political material, although the latter has increased over the years. Sometimes it makes gratuitous forays into politics by romanticizing revolutionaries at home or abroad, taking sides in the antinuclear-power movement, or attacking law enforcement agencies with allegations of brutality.

Rolling Stone has been described as "the *Wall Street Journal* of rock music." It does promote rock above all else, with an intensity that is more akin to religious zeal than loyalty, reporting each new excess in theatrics, drugs, sex or sheer absurdity as if it were unfolding the revealed truth. It celebrates the stars and their "groupie" camp-followers as if they were a priesthood with a retinue of acolytes. It portrays the frequent deaths among rock stars, whatever the cause, as tragedy bordering on martyrdom. It is thus not surprising that the magazine hacks away at essentially every value of the traditional culture, especially traditional religious beliefs. There is no room for competing belief systems. For *Rolling Stone,* rock is religion.

Whatever the publishers of the *Village Voice* and *Rolling Stone* may have intended, there have always been people in the underground press movement who have regarded these papers as more than mildly helpful.[17] Their influence in behalf of the counterculture has been welcome all along, and when the underground papers began to die out and the alternatives were still trying to find their way, the continuing success of these two publications gave heart to the "movement" people.

An Alternative Roll Call

Thus, in compiling the following list of general-topic alternative papers, both the *Village Voice* and *Rolling Stone* were added to those reported at the Seattle meeting and/or designated as alternatives in the five directories consulted:

Akwesane Notes, NY	*Aquarian,* NJ
Alaska Advocate	*Atlanta Gazette*
Ann Arbor Sun, MI	*Austin Sun,* TX

Berkeley Barb, CA
Big River News, CA
Borrowed Times, MT
Boston Phoenix, MA
Broken Barriers, LA
Bugle American, WI
Chicago Reader
Columbus Free Press, OH
Creative Loafing, GA
D.C. Gazette, DC
Door, CA
Drummer, PA
Fifth Estate, MI
Figaro, LA
First Issue, VT
Folly, PA
Free for All, WI
Free Venice Beachhead, CA
Gar, TX
Get Together, OH
Ghent Press, VA
Grass Roots, DC
Greenhouse, MO
Gris Gris, LA
Guardian, NY
Hartford Advocate, CT
Headhunter, TX
Iconoclast, TX
Independent Eye, OH
*Lancaster Independent
    Press*, PA
Lansing Star, MI
Liberation, NY
Lincoln Gazette, NB
Maine Times
Maui Sun, HI
Monday, Canada
Mt. Nebo Flash, OH
Mountain Views, AR
Mountain Newsreal, AZ
New Citizen, NY
New Frontier, NJ
New Haven Advocate, CT
New Rochelle Bugle, NY
New Times, IL

New Times (magazine), NY
New Times Weekly, AZ
New Unity, MA
North Carolina Anvil, NC
North Country Anvil, MN
North Star, CA
Northwest Passage, WA
Ocean Beach Peoples Rag, CA
Ozark Digest, AR
Pacific Sun, CA
People United, CA
Prairie Sun, IL
Primo Times, IN
Progressive, WI
Public Occurrence, VT
Radical America, MA
Rama, CA
Razzberry, OH
Realist, CA
Real Paper, MA
Rising Up Angry, IL
River City Review, TN
Rochester Patriot, NY
Rolling Stone, NY
San Diego Reader
San Francisco Bay Guardian
Sanity Now, CA
*Santa Barbara News
    & Review*, CA
Second City, IL
Seditions, CA
Seven Days, NY
Shelterforce, NJ
Southern Exposure, NC
Southern Patriot, KY
Southern Patriot, TN
Stamford Advocate, CT
Straight Creek Journal, CO
Take Over, WI
Texas Observer, TX
Twin Cities Reader
Utopian Eyes, CA
Valley Advocate, MA
Village Voice, NY
Washington Watch, WA

21

Weather Report, TX	*Win,* NY
Weekly, WA	*Wild Currants,* MN
White Lightning, NY	*Willamette Weekly,* OR

From the sample of these that we examined, it is apparent that, as the *Los Angeles Times* writer phrased it, "they have their spiritual roots" in the undergrounds. And, as he wrote, they are "anti-Establishment and generally to the left of the political center." He added, however, "But knee-jerk radicalism—and the sexual marketplace—are now largely gone from their pages." We found this not to be entirely accurate. If "knee-jerk radicalism" means reacting to events of the day with blasts of revolutionary rhetoric, as was typical of the underground papers, we readily agree—for they do not do that. If, on the other hand, it means a tendency to react automatically in the direction of the radical point of view, we cannot agree—for many do tend to do that. For example, the *Chicago Reader* devoted nearly three pages to mourning the "death of CAP," a radical-dominated community organizing activity in Chicago. The themes in this story were identical to one on the same subject, published in the "Independent Socialist" paper, *In These Times.* In another edition, the *Reader* gave a similar amount of space to a very warm and sympathetic treatment of the Alliance to End Repression, a coalition of left extremists whose "repression" target is the intelligence operations of law enforcement agencies.

As to the "sexual marketplace" having gone from their pages, the observation is also not accurate. The true underground papers carried very little in the way of sex advertising. The *L.A. Free Press* and the *Berkeley Barb* have always been exceptions, clearly intending to profit from sex advertising and often criticized for this practice by other papers. The more ideologically committed undergrounds shunned purely commercial sex ads from massage parlors, manufacturers of sexual paraphernalia, etc., but many did carry classified ads from individuals looking for sex partners. These were usually quite sophomoric, almost puritanical, however, when compared to the "swinger" ads appearing in some of today's alternative papers. There is nothing sophomoric about the classified ads for sexual activity in the modern alternative paper. For example, in *Figaro* of New Orleans and *Gris Gris* of Baton Rouge, there are ads openly specifying hetero-, homo-, or bisexual requirements, "married or single," or "couples to join us," etc.

In addition to the 99 papers listed above and the ones we have already touched on, there are four other general-topic alternatives worthy of specific mention:

In These Times, IL	*Paper Rose,* OR
Mother Jones, CA	*New Age,* NH

Oregon's *Paper Rose* is especially interesting. The June 1978 *Oregon Times* reports $253,861 in federal CETA funds allocated to this 48-page tabloid for 1978, and its own masthead reads "Sponsored by the Ecumenical Ministries of Oregon." From examination, it qualifies as an alternative with antibusiness themes and open sympathy for radical fugitives evading the law. The *Oregon Times* makes it known that its text is "intended to reach teen-agers" and to inform the "12-year-old Portland girl about tree-planters and the New Culture." It will also suggest to her the acceptability of sexual promiscuity, homosexual as well as heterosexual.

New Age is relatively new, a monthly in magazine format, published in Manchester, New Hampshire. It provides coverage of cultural and political change, and is engaged, according to its promotional ads, in "exploring in depth subjects that touch us all, such as sensuality, right livelihood, communities, and planetary healing."

Both *In These Times* and *Mother Jones* are relatively new. They are laden with leftist clichés and reach for mass audiences as "news" publications. *In These Times* calls itself a "socialist newspaper," but its contents reflect something further to the left than the term "socialist" suggests to the American public. Its ideology is comparable to the communist organizations which operate in Western European democracies. It is by no means a commercial venture, generally eschewing advertising and claiming to support itself largely on subscriptions, although the price is only $17.50 and it publishes weekly. It has a long list of endorsers from across the left side of the American political spectrum. It reports a circulation of over 12,000.

Mother Jones describes itself as "A Magazine for the Rest of Us" but it, too, is "socialist," and now published as a satellite operation of the Institute for Policy Studies (see page 13 above). Having begun publication in February 1976 as a slick-paper but rather amateurish magazine with no commercial advertising at all, it has improved markedly in appearance, toned down the underground character of its rhetoric and attracted an impressive amount of advertising from American corporations despite its consistent antibusiness editorial policy.

Liberation magazine was included in four of the alternative directories, although it is a monthly and quite political—a "magazine of solitary resistance to massed power," as one directory describes it. It does cover a variety of subjects, however, cultural as well as political. And it is written, edited and published by some of the same people who publish or write for other periodicals such as *In These Times* and *Seven Days*.

Indeed, *Seven Days* is an attempt to take the *Liberation* and *In These Times* brand of alternative material into the news-magazine field. Beginning publication in late 1976, *Seven Days* aspires "to reveal a world other than that presented in *Time* and *Newsweek*." It was established as a nonprofit periodical by the Institute for New Communications. It claims that it decided not to seek advertisements in order to limit costs, but that policy may be a necessity in view of the blatancy of its anticapitalism.

New Times,[18] also in news-magazine format, first appeared on October 19, 1973. It was founded by George Hirsch, who had previously founded *New York* magazine. Hirsch and his editor were both formerly with *Time-Life*, but were apparently inspired by the "looseness" they saw in the underground/alternative press. *Penthouse* described their intentions as:

> ". . . more than anything else to loosen up the slick impersonal cool of *Time*—to get behind, below and above the news with writers permitted to be unabashedly part of their own stories. They're hoping to bring the anti-bullshit liveliness of the underground press to a responsible, professional news medium. The result can be schizophrenic . . ."[19]

New Times is a slick-paper magazine, usually fat with corporate advertising, and usually filled with "anti-Establishment" and anticorporate articles: "Boardroom Bandits—America's Biggest Crooks," "The Marine Corps Builds Klansmen," "Anita Bryant's Holy War on Florida Gays," and "America Turns Right," are a few examples. Its covers often resemble those of rock music albums, in psychedelic colors and featuring grotesque or impudent pictures: a drawing of the back of President Kennedy's head being blown off, and a baby wearing an American flag as a diaper. The articles about "Establishment" personalities and institutions are usually in choppy, highly critical prose, and the interviewer scarcely permits his subject to get a word in. By contrast, the articles about people and organizations of the counterculture or the radical political left are smooth and sympathetic and these interviews are cast in folksy dialogue, with long passages quoted from the subject.

Yippie Abbie Hoffman, something of an anarchocommunist, and long-time fugitive from the law on a drug charge, was the subject of a laudatory cover story "from somewhere underground," and Sam Lovejoy, the radical antinuclear-power activist who sabotaged a 500-foot weather tower at a construction site in Massachusetts, was the subject of adulation in another cover story that was headlined: "Sam Lovejoy v. the Nuclear Juggernaut—Wherein our hero singlehandedly takes on the masters of nuclear destruction and their twin demon-hounds, Strontium 90 and Plutonium 239." In 1976 the magazine opened its cover and inner pages to the surviving members of the Hearst kidnap gang, providing them space to bemoan the martyrdom of their fellows killed in the Los Angeles shootout with police, and giving them eight to ten pages of dialogue among themselves in which to elaborate on their "basic belief in the necessity to use armed force to destroy U.S. corporate fascism."[20]

There are two more publications on the general-topic list that deserve comment. Neither of them would have fit in at Seattle, but both have been influential in the developmental history of the publications that were represented there: the *Realist* and *Win* magazine. The first was carried in three out of the five directories we consulted, and the second in four of them.

The *Realist* preceded the appearance of the underground papers by some six or seven years but it paved the way for their appearance, especially in the clever use of absurdity and irreverence as weapons against the cultural and political structures of the society. In his book, Glessing observed: "If the *Village Voice* broke the four-letter word barrier, the *Realist*, started by Paul Krassner in 1958, broke almost every other barrier."[21] Krassner, 26 when he founded the *Realist*, seems to have begun his journalistic career as a contributor to *Mad Magazine*. Recently he was named as publisher of Larry Flynt's sex magazine, *Hustler*. Glessing writes that Krassner began the *Realist* to produce a "magazine of irreverence in an era when most American institutions were considered above and beyond ridicule by traditional media."[22] In the course of its twenty-year history, the *Realist* has featured stories bearing such titles as "God Is Alive in Argentina," "The Sex Life of J. Edgar Hoover," "Computer Calculated Copulation," "I Was an Abortionist for the FBI," and "A Kick in the Inaugural Balls." Although the *Realist* has come out quite irregularly, sometimes going for months without an issue, it moved from an initial circulation of 600 to 150,000 by the end of the 1960s. The present circulation and publication arrangements are vague. This magazine began in New York and now shows a California address.

Win magazine is a publication of the War Resisters League, a pacifist organization begun in World War I that seems to have moved increasingly leftward and maintains a strong emphasis on unilateral U.S. disarmament. *Win* was first published in 1966, a prenuptial child of the eventual marriage of the "Old" and "New Left." Whereas the War Resisters League's brief newsletter, *WRL News*, began in the 1940s and remains somewhat formal and reserved in appearance, the pulp-paper *Win* magazine, which typically has twenty-four pages, exhibits the informality of the "New Left" and the casual lifestyle of the counterculture. Both publications are written and published by overlapping staffs in New York.

Win grew out of the underground press movement and found its sharp opposition to the Vietnam War to be the key to rapid growth. Its staff, like those of other papers, participated in various demonstrations and street and campus rallies. Indeed, one of *Win's* regular services was to disseminate instructions to the street people and campus activists about how to carry out a successful protest or demonstration. For the coordinated national protest of May 1, 1971, *Win* published a *Tactical Manual,* and distributed thousands of copies in advance of and during the Washington, D.C. demonstration which involved the blocking of streets and eventually led to mass arrests.

In addition to its principal focus upon the Vietnam War and then disarmament, *Win* has always included countercultural articles about art, literature, music and alternative living styles. It publishes several pages of a "Bulletin Board" listing radical, cultural and political meetings, rallies and educational activities throughout the country, and serves as a vehicle for the ideas, philosophy and ongoing programs of the political left. For a long time, *Win* has been run by David McReynolds, an avowed homosexual socialist who frequently writes about his choice of lifestyle as well as politics. Among the authors whose articles are written for or reprinted by *Win* are two men who have served on President Carter's speech-writing team. One, James Fallows, had written an antiwar article in the *Washington Monthly* that was reprinted in the June 30, 1977 *Win.* The other, Hendrik Hertzberg, not only has written articles for *Win* but was listed on its masthead as a part-time or supporting staff member of the magazine for several years, including much of 1977 after he had gone to work at the White House.[23]

When the Vietnam War ended, *Win* sought a new focus for its material. Before long, it assembled a number of issues under an umbrella project labeled the "Continental Walk for Disarmament and Social Justice." This ambulatory demonstration started in California and ended nine months later in Washington, D.C. Succeeding editions of the magazine reported on the progress of the venture, the organizations contacted and the issues added to its placards during the stopover rallies in the cities and towns along the way. As the walk ended in Washington in October, 1976, just shortly before the national elections, *Win* reported as participants more than twenty activist organizations and a list of issues almost as long as the walk. These included:

- Abolish the CIA and FBI

- Close all U.S. overseas bases

- Place corporations under worker and community control

- Halt the production of nuclear weapons

- Passage of the Humphrey-Hawkins Bill

- Day care legislation

- The Kennedy health bill

- Recognition and reconstruction aid for the "new" Vietnam
- Abolish laws relating to marijuana and homosexuality
- Establishment of a moratorium on nuclear-power plants
- Elimination of the death penalty

Almost immediately after this activity, *Win* turned its attention to the antinuclear-power movement and soon became a prominent chronicler of the demonstrations at Seabrook, New Hampshire; Diablo Canyon, California; Zion, Illinois; Rocky Flats, Colo., and so on. Predictably, *Win* and the War Resisters League set out to combine the antinuclear-power movement with the antinuclear-weapons movement which it had advocated for years. Recently, it has further extended the reach of its efforts to weaken the U.S. military, by insisting that "welfare rights" and "human needs" be met by transferring funds from the defense budget to welfare programs. This has been a recurrent theme in the pages of *Win*.

The publications considered thus far fall into the general-topic category, although as in the case of *Win*, there is a predominant political emphasis. In the balance of this study, publications have been clustered under various topics, but in many cases a periodical could justifiably be placed in one or more additional categories. For the most part, our designation has been made according to the classifications in the directories of the alternative press.

THREE

Alternative Politics

The Political Segment of the Alternative Press

The number of political publications is large, and the array of ideologies is broad. The computer-assisted compilation in the directory entitled *Alternative America* designates 73 publications as "political." The *Resources Catalogue,* prepared by Vocations for Social Change, a tightly-knit political collective, carries 80 in the category. The overlap between the two directories, however, is small. Together they provide more than 130 different entries. This is not surprising, considering the nature of the two sources. Vocations for Social Change is politically disciplined and parochial. It selects publications that serve, or at least do not conflict with, its own views and omits those with which it disagrees. In areas other than politics, its listing is more objective. *Alternative America* displays no such tendencies toward ideological selectivity, but does carry a number of publications that are marginal in other respects—that is, obscure, transistory or of little import-ance.[24]

In terms of circulation, the number of other papers that choose to advertise in its pages, the frequency of mention by other members of the alternative press and the stature of the writers, the following periodicals are judged to constitute the most significant segment of the political alternative press.

Black Panther, CA	*California Socialist*
Black Star, WI	*Call,* IL
Bulletin of the Atomic	*Challenge,* NY
Scientists, IL	*Daily World,* NY
Bulletin of Concerned Asian	*Dissent,* NY
Scholars, CA	*Gramma,* Cuba

[*Guardian*, NY]*
Industrial Worker, IL
Internationalism, NY
[*In These Times*, IL]
Libertarian Connection, CA
LSM News, CA
Marxist Perspectives, NY
Match, AZ
Militant, NY
Monthly Review, NY
[*Mother Jones*, CA]
Moving On, IL
NACLA Newsletter, NY
News & Letters, MI
Newsletter of the Democratic Left, NY
New Socialist, CO
New Unionist Newsletter, MA
Other Side, PA
Peoples World, CA
Philadelphia Solidarity, PA
Progressive, WI
[*Radical America*, MA]
Radical Religion, CA

Resistance, CA
Review of Radical Political Economics, NY
Revolution, IL
Root & Branch, MA
Science for the People, CA
[*Seven Days*, NY]
Socialist Review, CA
Socialist Tribune, WI
Sojourners, DC
Spark, MI
State and Mind, MA
Tricontinental News, NY
War Resisters League News, NY
Weekly People, CA
[*Win*, NY]
Worker, OR-WA
Workers Power, MI
Workers Vanguard, NY
Workers World, NY
Workforce, CA
Working Papers for a New Society, MA

*throughout this study, when a publication has already been placed in one category, it appears in brackets in any additional listings.

It may be helpful to indicate the general political orientation of these publications according to the political subcategories which we, for convenience, have designated: anarchy, libertarianism, democratic left-ism, theoretical Marxism, socialism, communism, and revolutionary internationalism. There are, however, some publications which justify separate treatment because they reflect the advocacy of radical politics within the framework of different vocational fields: the sciences and professions, labor and religion.

Three publications in the list reflect a commitment to *anarchism*: *Black Star*, published in Milwaukee, *Match*, published in Tucson, Arizona, and the *Industrial Worker*, published in Chicago. All three belonged to the Underground Press Syndicate and are still listed as belonging to the Alternative Press Syndicate. The first two of these publications are part of the Social Revolutionary Anarchist Federation, which has small affiliates in probably ten American cities and four or five Canadian ones. Although they usually muster no more than 100 participants at their occasional national meetings, their basic philosophy of Bakuninian anarchism, especially as interpreted by professor Herbert Marcuse and psychoanalyst Franz Fanon, has had an important influence upon the "New Left." As Brian Crozier has observed in his book, *A Theory of Conflict,* the Bakunins of the world "do not achieve revolutions, but they do create revolutionaries."[25] The *Industrial Worker* is the paper of the Industrial Workers of the World, an anarchosyndicalist organization that is now of marginal influence.

Libertarian organizations and libertarian publications are difficult to classify. The introductory paragraph to the "Libertarian" section of Muller and Spahn's *From Radical Left to Extreme Right* is illustrative of the problem:

"Libertarian periodicals stress the importance of personal liberty but do not necessarily oppose governmental power, as anarchists do. They do oppose immoral and coercive governments, especially those that start wars and exploit minorities. Libertarians cannot be neatly pigeonholed as leftist or rightist. They include those advocating laissez-faire private enterprise, less governmental control, and private ownership even of roads and police systems. Because they dislike direction by the state, they do not believe in salvation through socialism or economic planning, but they are not militantly anticommunist. The Young Americans for Freedom publication is in this chapter because its major motivation is to oppose government action that deprives individuals of their liberty; insofar as it endorses free trade and the need for an army, police and judicial system, it is close to the conservatives."[26]

Young Americans for Freedom is not listed in any of the five alternative directories consulted. Nor are there any other organizations that seem comparable in philosophy. In addition to some labeled merely "libertarian," there are organizations and publications cited as "libertarian anarchist," "libertarian socialist," and even "libertarian communist." Of those classified as merely "libertarian," *Philadelphia Solidarity* and *Libertarian Connection* seemed typical. The former is actually a distribution point for the British Solidarity publications leaning toward anarchy, and the latter seems to be utopian.

Under "democratic left" would fall the monthly *Newsletter of the Democratic Left* and the bimonthly magazine, *Dissent,* both published in New York City, and the monthly magazine, the *Progressive,* published in Madison, Wisconsin, which made headlines with its efforts to publish the formula for the hydrogen bomb. The *Newsletter of the Democratic Left* may be the most influential. It is the organ of the Democratic Socialist Organizing Committee whose members must occupy legislative and/or administrative posts in government at the local, state and national levels. The June 1976 edition of the *Newsletter of the Demo-*

cratic Left was flagged as a "Special Democratic Convention issue," and began:

> "If there was ever any doubt about the subject—and frankly there was not—the 1976 Democratic platform shows why the Democratic nominee must be elected in November. The Democrats have taken a progressive stand on critical domestic issues like full employment, national health care and tax reform. And although the Cold Warriors in the Party managed to insert some rhetoric and even some substance of their position, the platform is basically committed to détente. For these reasons, among many others, the democratic Left should work enthusiastically for the Democratic ticket during this campaign . . ."[27]

In subsequent paragraphs, this article explained that among other reasons that the "democratic Left" should support the ticket is that the presidential candidate was a Washington outsider and did not have "a blueprint for his Presidency in his pocket." There would be ample opportunity for input.

The article was written by Michael Harrington, author and university instructor, who has chaired the Democratic Socialist Organizing Committee since its founding in 1973, and has edited its newsletter almost as long. A year after he had written the article in his own newsletter, the quite-far-left magazine, *Mother Jones,* quoted him as telling "the convention of the New Democratic Coalition, the reform wing of the Democratic Party":

> "Carter hasn't done anything really horrendous. He will. But any time you get furious and say it didn't make any difference who won, bite your tongue. It makes a difference. If Carter has an inadequate full employment policy, as I think he does, at least we're discussing what *kind* of a full employment policy and not the idiotic question of whether there should be one."

He is said to have warmed to his topic later, and *Mother Jones* continued:

> " 'I think that we should offer Jimmy Carter our hand'—Harrington splays his fingers—'to help him fulfill the promises he made. And if he doesn't take our hand'—he clenches his fist—'we should give him a shove.'
> And so, with the politician's glad-hand and the revolutionist's fist, Michael Harrington has embarked upon a contradictory quest to bring socialism to America by the ballot box. Who is the man, and how much chance does he have?"[28]

Here, *Mother Jones* injects a footnote of caution against confusing the speaker with another Michael Harrington, a Democratic Representative from Massachusetts who "happens to be one of the small group

31

of liberal members of Congress sympathetic to some of socialist Harrington's ideas." This "socialist Harrington" has written seven books, including: *Socialism, The Other America, The Twilight of Capitalism,* and *Toward a Democratic Left.* He is fifty, but still called a "bright young socialist" by leftist elders like *Dissent* editor, Irving Howe. He gained wide attention in 1963 with his book on poverty, *The Other America.* It is said to have sold two million copies worldwide. *Mother Jones* claims Walter Heller, then chairman of the Council of Economic Advisers, put a copy into President Kennedy's hands, and "When LBJ declared war on poverty, Harrington was spirited off to Washington and found himself circulating memos to the President via Sargent Shriver."

All of this illustrates the concept of "working within the system" to change it—to an alternative. The alternative represented in the *Newsletter of the Democratic Left* tries to steer a course between liberalism, which it contends must arrive eventually at socialism, and existing forms of Marxist government, none of which it believes to be true to Marxist ideals. Irving Howe of *Dissent,* a closely associated magazine, is quoted as saying of the Democratic Socialist Organizing Committee: "My perspective is that of an American Fabian Society, a socialist group, that works within the Democratic Party and performs certain intellectual tasks but is not itself a party."[29]

The *Progressive* reported on a conference on "The American Political Economy in Crisis," held in April of 1975 in New York and co-sponsored by the Democratic Socialist Organizing Committee (DSOC) and the New American Movement. The article noted that the two organizations had a common ancestry, having risen from the ruins of the Students for a Democratic Society after its demise in 1969. The New American Movement has continued its militancy in the 1970s, and still calls "for direct action and mass anticorporate organizing, for new insurgency in the trade union movement" and for continuing aggressive action against "American intervention in the Third World." The DSOC, on the other hand, "stressed the importance of their work in the Democratic Party, the importance of legislative work and the need to build bridges to mainstream forces in the unions and politics." Both organizations agreed that there was need for dialogue between the advocates of political work and those of direct action.[30]

This "dialogue" is not a recent development. The DSOC is a recurrent topic in the pages of the *Militant,* and has sided with the *Militant's* parent group, the Trotskyite Socialist Workers Party (SWP) in its court action to force the Attorney General to provide the SWP with the government's documentation of the informers who had reported on its activities. The DSOC is listed as a "resource" in the *Corporate Action Guide,* an activists' manual for the type of "mass anticorporate organizing" advocated by the New American Movement.

The influence wielded by DSOC and its *Newsletter of the Democratic Left* is made clear in a *Mother Jones* article:

"DSOC started with 200 members, mostly the antiwar renegades from the old Socialist Party (which had followed its proletariat, the AFL-CIO, straight into Cold War politics) plus liberal trade unionists. Its membership rolls have swelled to 2,000 people. It has picked up impressive supporters. To cite a few: Kenneth Arrow, Nobel laureate in economics at Harvard; feminist Gloria Steinem; Robert Dahl, professor of political science at Yale; Victor Gotbaum, a top official of the American Federation of State, County and Municipal Employees; Georgia State Senator Julian Bond; and Rep. Ron Dellums (D-CA). Rep. John Conyers (D-MI) is a DSOC member in everything but name. And the United Auto Workers' Doug Fraser; Jerry Wurf, head of the AFSCME: and William W. Winpisinger, president of the International Association of Machinists, are veritable 'fellow travelers' of the DSOC cause. The group's asset is certainly the trade union officials, who comprise a full one-third of the membership. Its great weakness lies in its tiny smattering of blacks, who make up no more than 5 percent of the membership."[31]

As noted, a publication that reaches a select group of opinion leaders, as does the newsletter of the DSOC, has far more impact than might be supposed by a circulation of only a few thousand. The other two publications assigned to this subcategory, *Dissent* and the *Progressive,* have a similar impact, but larger circulations—more than 10,000 and 40,000 respectively.

Socialism

The next subcategory of alternative publications focused on political issues is designated "socialism," following the nomenclature used by the alternative directories, but there is no clear line of demarcation separating it from "the democratic left." For example, as noted previously, *In These Times* proclaims itself in its masthead, "The Independent Socialist Newspaper," but it is closely associated with the constituency of the DSOC and its *Newsletter of the Democratic Left.* Under "socialism" are listed: the *California Socialist, In These Times, Mother Jones,* the *New Socialist, Seven Days,* and *Working Papers for a New Society.*

The most important of the publications in this group in terms of influence on other members of the alternative media are judged to be *In These Times, Mother Jones,* and *Working Papers for a New Society.*

The *Militant* has described *In These Times* as "the latest stop in the political itinerary of a group of radicals around James Weinstein," its editor. Weinstein was editing the nondescript *Studies of the Left* back in the late 1960s. He closed that down to produce a more impressive magazine, at first called *Socialist Revolution*, but later retitled *Socialist Review*. He was a founder of the New American Movement and recruited a number of people from that organization to work for *In These Times*. Weinstein stated his goal as building "a sustained mass movement for socialism" on the heritage of the "old Socialist movement of 1900-19, the Communist movement inspired by the example of the Russian Revolution, and the 'new left'" of the 1960s. The next month he made explicit his opposition to capitalism:

> "CAPITALISM is a social system that organizes all human activity— 'economic,' 'political,' and 'social'—around the need to create and realize surplus value, around capitalist commodity production. Revolution requires a change in the principles that now determine all social decision-making. Such a transformation is possible only with the transfer of power over the political economy from the capitalist class to the proletariat, a transformation that establishes the conditions for developing social relations on a new basis. The revolutionary movement creates this potential by eliminating the capitalist class (which organizes all human activity toward the production and sale of commodities) and by replacing the capitalists by the producers (and consumers) themselves, who can then redefine work and organize production on the basis of socially determined need . . ."[32]

It is clear that *In These Times* continues to serve the objectives set forth in 1972. The promotional literature introducing *In These Times* to the public states as the intended purpose:

> ". . . to identify and clarify the struggles against corporate power now developing throughout American society, to bring to explicit consciousness their implicit *anticapitalism,* and to point out that a socialist democracy is the only means of attaining both equality and liberty under modern conditions."[33]

This literature also provides endorsements by writers and political figures, including a current U.S. Congressman, to the effect that there was "an urgent need for alternative forms of political education" of the American electorate such as that provided by *In These Times*.

The paper's first editorial carried a list of what it termed its "basic principles." The first two of these were:

> "Our overriding commitment is to democracy, to socialism as the means to its attainment, and to the inseparability of democracy and socialism in modern industrial society. We are convinced that

capitalism is irreconcilable with a democracy based on the indivisibility of liberty and equality."[34]

These principles have been dominant in the pages of *In These Times*—the "socialist" movement being the means for "forging unity against capitalism." Of late, the periodical has rejoiced that in the past few years, the organized labor movement has begun to go beyond "narrow collective bargaining" so that it is increasingly available for coalitions with ethnic minorities, women, consumers, and community organizations for moving into conflict with the "corporate investment system"—and the formation of alliances "for social goals against corporate aggrandizement." This movement "is just beginning to honeycomb the American body politic," the paper argues, and requires the mobilization of all elements to:

". . . elect new types of representatives to city councils, state legislatures, and Congress—representatives from the ranks of labor, women, blacks, and others who will champion the people's interests and popular sovereignty against corporate power . . ."[35]

The *Militant*, apparently jealous of its upstart leftist rival, charges that *In These Times* has no "roots in the working-class movement," but aligns itself with "the more liberal wing of top labor officialdom . . . Douglas Fraser of the United Auto Workers, William Winpisinger of the International Association of Machinists, and Jerry Wurf of the American Federation of State, County and Municipal Employees." The article goes on to note that there are "thirty-two chapters of *In These Times* associates, headed by Rep. John Conyers and author Studs Terkel."[36] Such a list of names could have continued with the forty "sponsors" shown on the *In These Times* masthead, including Georgia Senator Julian Bond; MIT professor and *Seven Days* columnist Noam Chomsky; director of Washington University's Center for the Biology of Natural Systems and antinuclear-power activist Barry Commoner; former People's Bicentennial Commission participant and current associate editor of the *Insurgent Sociologist,* University of California professor G. William Domhoff; Daniel Ellsberg, who became known for his part in the "Pentagon Papers" incident; DSOC chairman Michael Harrington; former California Communist Party leader Dorothy Healey; "New Left" mentor, professor Herbert Marcuse; People's Business (formerly "Bicentennial") Commission leader Jeremy Rifkin; and Institute for Policy Studies Fellow Derek Shearer.[37]

The list could have continued with Rep. Ron Dellums (D-CA) and the elder statesman of leftist journalists I. F. Stone, whose endorsements have appeared in display ads for the paper. And it could have included as heroes and heroines praised by *In These Times* such figures as: former Congresswoman Bella Abzug; Gar Alperovitz, Fellow of the

Institute for Policy Studies; Dennis Kucinich, mayor of Cleveland; Maggie Kuhn of the Gray Panthers; feminist Betty Friedan; Ken Cockrel, Marxist recently elected to the Detroit city council; Vernon Jordan; Hosea Williams; and Isabel Letelier, widow of Orlando Letelier, the murdered former member of the Allende government in Chile.

Perhaps the list of heroes and heroines should be extended even further. In response to a reader's letter questioning whom the paper had in mind when it spoke of the need for "moral authority" over the American socialist movement, *In These Times* editors wrote:

"When we wrote of moral authority we had in mind political leadership based on the public enunciation of principles and program. Like Thomas Jefferson, Fidel Castro, Rosa Luxemburg or maybe Abraham Lincoln, V. I. Lenin, Paul Robeson. More like that. Anyway, *In These Times* is not the American socialist movement, only a small part of it."[38]

On topical coverage, *In These Times* runs heavily toward labor unrest, anticorporate incidents and stories, public health care, abortions, welfare, full employment, antinuclear-power activism, prison conditions political upheavals and revolutions in other countries, leftist figures around the world and enthusiastic accounts of the prospects for Eurocommunism.

Another publication that requires special consideration in the socialist subcategory is *Mother Jones*—a slick-paper, $8\frac{1}{2} \times 11$ magazine printed in four colors. It began publication in February 1976 with 88 pages, of which one page could be considered "outside" advertising (from a radical women's organization in Berkeley), and a half page of classified advertising labeled "Public Interest." The September/October 1978 edition of the magazine had 72 pages of which $12\frac{1}{2}$ pages were display ads, some from nationally known business organizations and publishing houses, and 2 full pages of classified advertising, most of which is openly antibusiness or antireligious, and some of which is openly designated as Marxist, anticapitalist or revolutionary.[39] Between those two dates, 25 editions of this magazine were published, showing a steady increase in the amount of advertising and in the militancy on specific corporations and capitalism in general.

In the September 1978 edition, an editor wrote:

"If everything goes according to plan we will, sometime in 1979, become this country's first Left magazine in the last 35 years to break even ... In scorning the business world's values, too many radicals also tend to scorn its skills; so anyone running the business side of a radical institution has a doubly hard row to hoe. Over the last four years [staff member Richard] Parker has helped introduce the rest of us to everything from cost accounting to direct-mail advertising. He went out and found experts with the needed specialized experience . . . he taught us all how to use a line-item, month-by-month budget; and he negotiated the growth strategies that have put us on the road to becoming a magazine financially supported by its readers. With this issue, Parker is leaving *MJ* [*Mother Jones* magazine] to move on to several new projects—one of which may be a book-publishing program in association with our parent organization, the Foundation for National Progress."[40]

Wherever the credit may lie, even the appearance of the magazine shows the touch of modern marketing techniques, and the mailers *Mother Jones* has sent out in the past two years are equal in quality to those of the most prosperous magazines of the country.[41]

At the end of its first six months of publication—that is, in September 1976—*Mother Jones* claimed a total paid circulation of 94,026—73,000 of which was in mail subscriptions, the rest in newsstand sales. Two years later as of October 1, 1978, total paid circulation was claimed to be 275,499—with 195,000 of these in subscriptions and nearly 80,000 in counter sales. In calendar year 1976 the reported free distribution averaged nearly 3,000. In 1978, the complimentary copies averaged 392. The circulation statement shows an annual subscription rate of $12, and the covers are now marked $1.50 for counter sales, but various special offers, including "charter subscriber" rights to the original introductory subscription rate, put the subscription prices more realistically at between $6 and $9 for the ten issues published each year.

The name *Mother Jones* comes, as is illustrated in the masthead of every issue of the magazine, from the labor-movement name of Mary Harris Jones who, from her late forties to her mid-nineties, was nationally known for her work as an organizer among, and spokeswoman for, mine workers. She was credited with helping to found the Industrial Workers of the World and was active in support of the Mexican Revolution. Once when she was introduced to a college audience as a "great humanitarian," she interrupted to shout, "No! I'm a hellraiser." The legend of Mother Jones has been a favorite among radical organizations and throughout the underground/alternative publications. A few years ago there was a Mother Jones Collective in Baltimore, a Mother Jones Revolutionary League in Madison, Wisconsin, and a Mother Jones commune in Berkeley. Now there is a Mother Jones Press, a women's printing shop in Massachusetts; a Mother Jones Food Co-op in Detroit; *Mother Jones Gazette,* described as a lesbian publication in Knoxville; as well as the *Mother Jones* magazine. The name was a natural for the group which began the task in the winter of 1975-76 of producing a slick-paper leftist publication in California. It was a name that would immediately communicate the nature of the publication to people familiar with the lore of the left.

The early issues of *Mother Jones* were rather crudely presented. The magazine format and the glossy paper did little to dispel the aura of underground press manifest in its pages in the coarse language and the unvarnished radical politics. The articles dwelt at length on the activities of "The Left," citing names of people and organizations that might call straying activists back to the ranks. There were favorable commentaries about the revolutionaries of the 1940s in China, the Viet Cong, the Castro regime in Cuba, the Palestinian guerrillas, and the communist elements in the Portuguese turmoil. Considerable attention was given to "gay rights" and to lesbianism, and a cover story dealt with children growing up in communes. There were broad attacks on conservatism, the intelligence function of law enforcement agencies and the national defense structure, and attempts to ridicule anticommunism. The bulk of the articles alternated between heavy-handed promotion of the political left and castigation of the political right. In the fifth issue, dated August 1976, a change was evident. The generalized polemics began to yield to direct attacks on established organizations and institutions, and the promotion of specific left-extremist causes and institutions.

In that issue, there was an article directed against the Bell Telephone system. The gist was that because the telephone companies make large profits, the consumers and telephone workers should run them instead of management. The focus was specific, aiming at a single corporation rather than abstract capitalism, but the line of reasoning remained one that would appeal only to those in tune with the political left. Thereafter, the editors turned to the far more sophisticated technique of justifying their attacks by allegations of immoral, unjust or criminal conduct as perceived within the traditional value system. Beginning with the September/October 1976 issue, containing an article alleging that the Mobil Oil Corporation was breaking the law, *Mother Jones* began the type of muckraking that has become its stock in trade. As the strategy has unfolded, it seems clear that the niceties of well-documented allegations are not a primary concern of the editors. *Mother Jones* claims no constructive intentions, but seems to relish the motto of its heroine, to "Raise Hell!"[42] Agitation seems to prevail over documentation.

The campaigns *Mother Jones* seems most pleased to have espoused are, according to its own promotional ads:

" 'Bust Your Boss' told the whole story of Mobil's illegal shipments of oil to Rhodesia during the embargo, including a daring ploy by a group of activists, an insider's leak and a secret rendezvous at Penn Station to get the information out." (Ad in Sept./Oct. 1977 edition, article in Sept./Oct. 1976.)

" 'A Case of Corporate Malpractice.' If you think you know the full story of the Dalkon Shield, the IUD that has killed at least 17 women, look again. Here is our own reconstruction of how lies, shaky statistics and sheer hucksterism helped a dubious medical invention gross millions for its corporate backers." (Table of Contents blurb and article in Nov. 1976 edition.)

"The Myth of the Green Revolution." (A group of three articles.)

" 'Eating Oil.' From the kitchens of Amoco comes petroleum protein. Fifteen million pounds a year end up in food products."

"Still Hungry after All These Years." This article shows how Del Monte, United Brands and the like are the real beneficiaries of the so-called "Green Revolution"—and of the food aid the U. S. sends a-broad.

" 'The Day of the Locust.' Just in case we're not getting enough chemicals in our food already, Chevron and other companies are promoting 'no-plow farming,' where huge doses of powerful chemicals take the place of tilling the soil." (Ad in Dec. 1978 edition.)

" 'Pinto Madness.' For seven years the Ford Motor Company manufactured cars in which it knew hundreds of people would burn to death. A cost-benefit analysis that assigned a dollar value to human life was a major factor in Ford's decision not to modify the car. The article was a major journalistic coup of 1977, resulting in the largest recall in automotive history and a National Magazine Award for *Mother Jones.*" (Ad in Dec. 1978, article in Sept./Oct. 1977.)

" 'The Baby Bottle Scandal.' A woman gives birth in Guatemala or in Nigeria, or Pakistan. At the hospital, a white-uniformed person who looks like a nurse gives her free samples of infant formula. She bottle feeds her baby for a few days, and her own breast milk dries up. Then she discovers that a month's supply of formula costs up to half of her family's income. She can't afford it. What happens? A searing report on the billion-dollar outrage American and European business has perpetrated on the Third World." (Table of Contents blurb, and article in Dec. 1977 edition.)

The last item above supports a boycott campaign being operated out of the offices of the National Council of Churches in New York, and urges readers to send congressmen and senators a copy of the article and a claim that "we need legislation" to stop "aggressive infant-formula sales in the Third World," with copies to the Nestlé Company and Bristol-Myers.

Whereas the attack on Bell Telephone seemed to create little if any stir, those subsequently launched or endorsed by *Mother Jones* have all generated significant repercussions. The "Pinto Madness" matter which it claims to have instigated is one the Ford Motor Company is not likely to forget. The Sept./Oct. 1977 edition of *Mother Jones* carried as its cover story an eleven-page article on the Pinto automobile which it alleged to be a fire hazard. The cover photo showed a screaming woman in a burning car. It claimed that the article was based on "secret documents showing that for seven years the Ford Motor Company sold cars in which it knew hundreds of people would needlessly burn to death." *Mother Jones* continued to "update" its charges and their results in succeeding issues. In addition to whatever fear and ill-will derived from this campaign, there have been a series of lawsuits, pressure for massive recall of automobiles, and demands from some quarters for the criminal prosecution of some of the company's executives.

This series of sensational articles against products and corporations, featuring more invective than documentation, includes some campaigns that seem to have been initiated by *Mother Jones,* and others that are simply repeated and orchestrated attacks launched from other quarters. The Nestlé boycott, rising from the alleged impropriety in introducing prepared baby formulas into nonindustrial cultures, is an example of the latter. The J. P. Stevens boycott and the campaigns against the Bank of America and Coors Beer are others.

The pattern that began to emerge in the August and September 1976 editions has come fully into view. Some of the motives and methods behind this pattern have come into view also. They deserve more attention than they have received. The article so curtly headlined "Bust Your Boss" and its sources are worthy of careful examination. The story is not a long one, only about 2500 words. Some 580 words are devoted to a dramatization of the "secret rendezvous at Penn Station" where "Jeremy Rifkin, head of the People's Bicentennial Commission" is alleged to have received the "insider's leak" that finally brought the Mobil scandal to the surface." Four hundred words are given over to a folksy, though not very accurate, description of the People's Bicentennial Commission. Some 350 words were allocated to a geoeconomic discourse on Rhodesia and South Africa. Over 600 words were used to convey Rifkin's criticism of the mass media for not publicizing the "exposé" given out at the press conference he held. Only 479 words were devoted to the allegations against Mobil, with no accompanying reproductions of documents, memos or anything else.

Almost two-thirds of the story is about the "People's Bicentennial Commission," or "PBC" as it is spoken of usually; the cash rewards it had offered to get derogatory information about corporations from people on the payroll; the secretive meeting this ploy produced, and PBC leader Jeremy Rifkin's displeasure with the press for not taking him seriously. It should be noted that the story claims Mobil "attacked PBC as an extremist group." If it did, Mobil was not alone in the attack. Although Rifkin and the PBC enjoyed months of favorable attention from the media, the red, white and blue bunting with which it had draped itself finally wore thin, exposing a less than savory undertaking.

Although the *Chicago Tribune* had reported *some favorable* comments about PBC earlier, the *Tribune's* editors wrote on December 20, 1975:

> "We had hoped that something called the People's Bicentennial Commission would sink long ago under the weight of its own absurdities. But, alas, it has captured the lion's share of Bicentennial publicity . . .
>
> There is nothing wrong with criticizing big business; we do it on this page on occasion. But when sombody undertakes to denounce the whole system — and poses as a patriot in the process — it is prudent to examine his credentials. The credentials of the People's Bicentennial Commission are abominable.
>
> We have searched its literature in vain for a list of members of the Commission. It is no more a 'people's' organization than the People's Republic of China; and if this implies an affinity for communism, it is not accidental. The Commission's chief (and for all we have seen, only) spokesman is Jeremy Rifkin, a tireless 30-year-old who seems to specialize in shadowy commissions . . .
>
> The Commission's best known Illinois backer is probably John Rossen, a Chicago theater owner who has often been identified as a former Communist Party organizer and who headed a pro-Castro rally here in 1961. Last year Rep. Richard Ichord, then chairman of the House Committee on Internal Security, traced the conception of the PBC to Mr. Rossen. Both he and Mr. Rifkin deny that they collaborated in this, but they did collaborate as co-authors of a book entitled *How To Commit Revolution American Style,* published in 1973."

The tracing of the conception of PBC to which the *Tribune* refers indicates very definite "roots" in the underground press. Contrary to the *Mother Jones* story's assertion that "after all, PBC had been founded on the danger of sheer corporate size in America," it was founded as a far-left *alternative* to the traditional celebrations planned for the nation's birthday. The project had been proposed and described in detail, in first the *New Patriot* and then the *New American Movement* — both underground papers — by John Rossen and Jeremy Rifkin respectively. Rossen, in his own sixties in the 1960s, but nevertheless thoroughly involved in those elements of the Students for a Democratic Society that produced the terrorist Weatherman organization, originated the idea for PBC and coined an expression which embodied its basic strategy: "The way to radicalize America is to Americanize radicalism." He elaborated on this theme by presenting in his underground paper, the *New Patriot*, quotations and symbols from the America of the 1770s that could be used alongside those of modern radicalism—some of *his* very *drawings* later being used in PBC literature. Jeremy Rifkin, a founding member of the SDS offspring, the New American Movement, and now a sponsor of the alternative newspaper *In These Times*, picked up the idea from Rossen and wrote a blueprint for it which was published in his organization's underground paper, *New American Movement*. In the November 1971 edition of that paper he made it completely clear that PBC was to be a tool for attracting new recruits into left movements and for getting media exposure of radical left ideas. He wrote:

> ". . . it makes no sense for the New Left to allow the defenders of the system the advantage of presenting themselves as the true heirs and defenders of the American revolutionary tradition. Instead, the revolutionary heritage must be used as a tactical weapon to isolate the existing institutions and those in power . . ."[43]

> "Aside from engaging large numbers of people for the first time—who might not feel comfortable relating directly to NAM [the New American Movement], the People's Commissions provide a unique forum for mass media exposure over the next four years. This mechanism could be used to raise political awareness and to promote NAM and other radical activities and demands."[44]

Since he was writing in a paper in which he was speaking to fellow ideologues, he left no doubt as to what the left or radicalism meant to him. In the same article from which the above passages were taken, he said:

> "A genuine understanding of revolutionary ideals is what links Thomas Paine, Sam Adams and Benjamin Rush, and the American people with Lenin, Mao, Che, and the struggles of all oppressed people in the world . . ."[45]

When Rifkin took PBC to the American public he used some of the same material that had been in those underground papers—indeed, the paragraph from which the above came—but he carefully removed the references to "Lenin, Mao, Che," etc., changed such phrases as "our *revolutionary* ideals" to "our *democratic* ideals" and went to press.

In fact, some of his sanitized material was published in the *New York Times*. That paper was initially very receptive to PBC's ideas and writings—sanitized as we have indicated above, of course—but this receptive attitude changed abruptly over the "ploy" *Mother Jones* mentioned. On May 6, the *Times* editorialized:

> "When the People's Bicentennial Commission initially appeared to be taking aim at some of the more commercial and hypocritical manifestations of the nation's 200th anniversary observance, such puncturing of stuffed-shirt chauvinism did not seem a bad idea. But PBC's lofty proclamations about a 'reaffirmation of the principles of democracy,' have long since been superseded by sophomoric pranks.
>
> More recently, PBC's transparent anticapitalist bias has led it to resort to dangerously dirty tricks. The group has addressed a form letter to 10,000 secretaries of corporate executives, offering a $25,000 reward to any recipient who provides 'concrete information that leads directly to the arrest, prosecution, conviction and imprisonment of a chief officer . . . for criminal activity relating to corporate operations.'
>
> Thus this pseudoliberal organization has now stooped to that oldest of totalitarian subversions—the organizing of internal spy systems in family, business or community . . ."[46]

The *Times'* mention of "spy systems in family . . ." in this last sentence was no doubt a reference to the fact that PBC had also mailed cassette tapes to the wives of a number of corporate executives, urging them to become informers—for "moral and spiritual reasons." On these tapes a male voice, with the introductory comment that "We are the People's Bicentennial Commission," rolls out in measured, often dramatic and near-threatening tones, the following:

> "Dear Friend,
>
> We are communicating with you because your husband is one of the top business leaders in the country. For that reason we think you should listen carefully to what we have to say.
>
> No doubt you are aware of the recent revelations of widespread corruption and criminality in the corporate boardrooms. It started with the Watergate investigations when seventeen major American corporations were forced to admit illegal contributions and payoffs. But that was merely the tip of the iceberg.
>
> During the past three years corporate scandals have reached epic proportions. ITT was discovered to have worked for the overthrow of the democratically elected government in Chile. Scores of American multinational corporations have been implicated by the Justice Department, the FCC and the Treasury Department in scandals involving hundreds of millions of dollars in bribes, kickbacks, and payoffs in this country and abroad.

Lockheed has already admitted paying out $202 million, Northrop $30 million, Exxon $27 million, Tenneco $12 million. Investigators maintain that before the scandals subside hundreds of American corporations will be exposed for similar practices.

This unprecedented criminal epidemic had led one FCC official to remark, QUOTE: 'We now see corporate misdeeds being carried on in business to an extent that it is sickening.' UNQUOTE.

We think these corporate scandals put a special responsibility on your family to ask some probing questions of your husband, because it is no longer possible to argue that the rampant corporate criminality represents merely isolated incidents or the aberrational behavior of a few perverted individuals.

In fact, a recent survey by the prestigious Conference Board found that over half the executives surveyed said that they would not hesitate to make the same kind of payoffs if they felt it would help their company make a sale. Have you ever asked your husband which half of that survey he falls in?

Have you ever asked him if he or his colleagues, or his firm have ever been involved in *criminal* activity? Would your husband inform the authorities if he was aware of illegal conduct among his own friends and associates? Would you inform the authorities if you uncovered such information?

For too long, our nation has applied a double standard of justice on questions of corporate crime versus street crime. The American people should no longer allow business leaders to hide under a veil of a corporation when it comes to the proper administration of justice.

We are deeply concerned over the criminal rampage that major corporation leaders have embarked on. The new ethic of business immorality is poisoning the social fabric of our country and *it must be stopped,* before it pervades every aspect of our life and turns us into a nation of cutthroats and thieves.

The government is doing little or nothing to prosecute criminality in the corporate boardroom. The politicians are virtually silent about the matter. The courts show little inclination to do more than slap a few wrists at best, or at worst, turn away from the problem altogether.

This leaves the responsibility up to you. Why? Because moral conduct starts with the family unit. You and your family should be taking the necessary steps now to make sure that your own house is in order spiritually and morally. Isn't it time to start discussing the issues we've raised in this communication openly with your husband and your family? What better time to begin than when your husband comes home this evening for dinner.

In the Spirit of '76
We are the People's Bicentennial Commission"

It is not surprising that some of the women who received this tape in the mail were upset. There was no identification of the speaker, not even a mention of what locality he was speaking from—just that last line, intoned almost ominously, "We are the People's Bicentennial Commission." And, for all the moralizing and the self-righteous inflection in the pronunciation of the word *criminality*, the tape had been put into the mail by an organization that was in itself the essence of fraud. The *Chicago Tribune* was correct, it was an organization that had no "Commission," and one whose use of the word "People's" was more in the sense of that in the People's Republic of China—or in the People's Democratic Republic of this or that in some other totalitarian corner of the world—than anything else. And it was an organization whose claim to the use of the word "bicentennial" was probably most aptly described in the title of a report to a U.S. Senate subcommittee on Internal Security, "The Attempt to Steal the Bicentennial."[47]

The staff of *Mother Jones* knew all of this. They were frequently involved in the exchange of material with a host of leftist organizations in Washington, including PBC. Indeed, the magazine's choice of a title for the story in the Sept./Oct. 1976 issue of the magazine was "Let's Make a Deal." In subsequent promotional ads, the title was changed to "Bust Your Boss." It happens that during the month that the Washington, D.C. office of the PBC was mailing the tapes to the wives of corporate executives and the $25,000 form letter to their secretaries, a weekly tabloid named *Newsworks* was running a "Why I Hate My Boss" essay contest in the same city. This paper—properly classified as underground despite *Mother Jones'* designation of it as "an alternative weekly"—used a full-page display ad to urge all its readers, not just secretaries, to:

"Tell the world what a shit your boss really is . . .

Send it to us and we'll help you wage that vendetta. *Newsworks*, that esteemed conduit of dissatisfactions, wants to help you . . .

Our editorial staff will judge the essays on the basis of venality, corruptive influences, the originality of alienation, and hatefulness . . ."[48]

The close ties between these two publications are manifest. During the summer and fall of 1976, several of the staff members of *Newsworks* moved to *Mother Jones*. *Newsworks'* encouragement to corporate employees to reveal damaging information about their employers was even worked into its masthead. "Do you find yourself reading those xeroxed copies of secret interoffice memoranda? . . . send your hot tips to us."[49] And its pages repeatedly indicated working relationships with both PBC and *Mother Jones*. However, the outreach of *Mother Jones* extends much further, with numerous direct and indirect relationships into the standard press as well as the surviving underground papers.

A tabulation of the credentials of the writers appearing in *Mother Jones* and of the organizations favorably featured in its articles suggests that more than thirty publications, as well as twenty activist or purely political organizations, have some degree of formal contact with *Mother Jones*. The publications range from left-extremist alternatives, such as *Guardian*, to standard magazines and newspapers, such as *The New Yorker* and the *Los Angeles Times*.

One of the current contributing editors came to *Mother Jones* from Boston's *Real Paper*, where he had been associate editor and a Nieman Fellow at Harvard. One of the members of the *Mother Jones* editorial board is described as Washington correspondent for the *Boston Phoenix*, a contributor to the *Progressive*, as well as formerly of the now-defunct *Newsworks*. Another individual who has written for *Mother Jones* is reported to write for both the Boston *Real Paper* and *Phoenix*, and is shown by *In These Times* to be its bureau chief in Boston. Another is listed as a writer or columnist for both the *Real Paper* and the *Phoenix* and as a contributing editor to *Rolling Stone*. The music editor of the *Real Paper* had an article in *Mother Jones*, as did a film critic from Marin County, California's *Pacific Sun*, and a reporter for a Boston TV station, who is also a contributor to the *Real Paper*. One free-lance writer with an article in *Mother Jones* is credited also with having pieces in the *New York Times Magazine*, the *Village Voice*, and *Redbook*. Another is cited as writing for the *New York Times* and the alternative magazine *New Times*, as well as *Mother Jones*. Two contributing editors to the *Texas Monthly* have articles in *Mother Jones*. One member of the *Mother Jones* editorial board was once an editor of the now-defunct radical magazine *Ramparts*. He was also at one time a Berkeley representative of the Marxist collective that published one of the directories we consulted, Vocations for Social Change. In that capacity, he was listed in an earlier directory as being available to offer "free advice to movement groups about press conferences, press releases and how to use the media . . ." One of those listed on the *Mother Jones* masthead formerly wrote for *Ramparts*. He is now West Coast editor for *Working Papers for a New Society*, is a sponsor of *In These Times*, is reported to have been a "part of Jerry Brown's administration," is a Fellow at the Institute for Policy Studies, and regularly involved in the annual National Conference on Alternative State and Local Public

Policies.[50]

A summary of the affiliations of seventy-six persons who work for or have been featured prominently in *Mother Jones* follows. Periodicals are in italics. Activist organizations are not. The numbers following each item indicate how often a relationship with *Mother Jones* was identified in the tabulation.

ACORN[51] 1
Boston Phoenix 1
*Bulletin of Concerned
    Asian Scholars* 1
Center for Cuban Studies 3
Democratic Socialist
    Organizing Committee 3
Dissent 2
Dollars & Sense 4
Esquire 2
Fair Share 1
Gay Sunshine 1
Great Speckled Bird 2
Guardian 1
Indochina Resource Center 2
Industrial Workers of
    the World 2
Inquiry 1
Institute for
    Policy Studies 18
In These Times 17
Liberation News Service 3
Los Angeles Times 1
Marxist Perspectives 2
Midwest Academy 2
Mobilization for Survival 3
Ms. (magazine) 2
NACLA Newsletter 2
Nader Organizations 4
National Conference for
    Alternative State and
    Local Public Policies 10
Newsworks 5
New Times 6
New West 1
The New Yorker 1

New York Review of Books 1
New York Times 3
Other Side 2
Pacific Sun 1
People's Bicentennial
    Commission 3
Progressive 2
Ramparts 5
Real Paper 10
Redbook 1
Red Cent Collective 1
Rolling Stone 5
*Santa Barbara News
    & Review* 2
Saturday Review 1
Science in the
    Public Interest 1
Seven Days 2
Students for a
    Democratic Society 6
Texas Monthly 2
Texas Observer 2
Union of Radical
    Political Economists 2
US-China Peoples
    Friendship Association 1
Village Voice 4
Washington Monthly 1
Weathermen 1
Win (magazine) 2
Witness 2
*Working Papers for
    a New Society* 6
Youth Against War
    and Fascism 1

Brief information on publications and organizations in this list, not covered elsewhere in this, appears in Footnote 51.

Since *Mother Jones* and *Working Papers for a New Society* were instigated by the Institute for Policy Studies which has its roots in the Students for a Democratic Society, as did the New American Movement which was instrumental in establishing *In These Times,* the strong ties between these operations are not surprising, but the extent of communications and interactions among the alternative press and its supporting bodies reflected in this listing is significant.

The interactions here noted reflect what radical activists and organizers commonly call "the movement." This term may be unfamiliar to the general public. People recognize such expressions as "the civil rights movement," "the antiwar movement," "the women's movement," and the "antinuclear-power movement," but the most common expression within the underground/alternative publications is simply "the movement."

The old underground papers were full of such references. For example, in 1972, *Modern Utopian,* published by the Alternatives Foundation, described the efficacy of communes with this expression: "Communal living has proved to be a successful alternative to the single family unit, and has provided valuable resources to *the movement.*" [Emphasis added.] The *Source Catalogue,* an alternatives directory, in listing the volume *From Radical Left to Extreme Right,* states: "This reference was not written by *the movement* [Emphasis added] but is one of a very few attempts to list and annotate these periodicals." The Boston Student Collective's *The Organizer's Manual,* published by Bantam Books, lists the phone numbers of "Movement Lawyers" and has a section entitled "General Movement Organizations."[52] *Win* magazine headlined an article about the antinuclear-power protests in New Hampshire: "The Movement at Seabrook."

The former staff member of *Newsweek,* Laurence Leamer, tried to describe "the movement" in his book, *The Paper Revolutionaries.* His research included visits to underground newspapers and radical organizations across the country. The *Washington Star's* review of his book included this passage:

"The Movement that grew up in this country during the 1960s was, of course, more than a youth movement. Laurence Leamer describes it as 'an amorphous, variegated clan, whose only common link is allegiance to the heady pastiche of pot, peace, Panthers, rock, antiwar, anti-imperialism, anarchism and Marxism . . . No one could possibly devise a structure to encompass this Movement. It would have to be a grand geodesic dome fitted together from pieces of Marx, Freud, Zen, Artaud, Kesey, Lenin, Leary, Ginsberg, Che, Gandhi, Marcuse, Laing, Fidel and Lao Tzu strung with the black banners of anarchy to which the sayings of Chairman Mao have been neatly embroidered and with a 40-watt rock amplifier strapped to the top—a gaudy, mind-blowing spectacle and an impossible intellectual synthesis.'"[53]

Other writers have found what some have called the "freak shows" within the counterculture to be similarly distracting. However, if they had trouble discovering synthesis in it all, a Marxist theorist did not. Writing at about the same time Leamer was doing the research for his book, Irwin Silber, cultural commentator and senior political pundit on the staff of the left-extremist *Guardian,* wrote in his *The Cultural Revolution: A Marxist Analysis:*

"Since capitalism no longer conforms to social necessity, its entire cultural codification—its art, religion, politics, philosophy, moral code, lifestyles, all that we call the superstructure of society—has become intellectually barren.

But the social atrophy of the capitalist system is insufficient, by itself, to bring about its destruction. The bourgeoisie is a tenacious ruling class and capitalism holds on—past its time . . . But it cannot stave off the ideological contradictions which have disrupted its cultural apparatus.

Out of this has come the cultural upheaval of the 1960s. We are all familiar with the specific manifestations of the process: dropping of sexual inhibitions, psychedelic drugs, a new concern with personalized and individualized experience as opposed to the intellectual experience, the diminishing value of material goals and a repugnance for artificially induced luxuries, the obliteration of conscious patterns of racial and religious prejudice, a general lack of respect for all forms of authority, an impatience with outmoded cultural values, the accelerating destruction of such social institutions as marriage, the family, the established church and hierarchies in general, etc."[54]

The societal impact of this phenomenon which an author from the dominant culture was unable to define is diagnosed as terminal illness by one of the arch-spokesman of radical orientation.

In an article in *Barron's* entitled "For Socialist Alternatives: A Radical Think Tank Is Working Within the System," David Kelley wrote:

"The Movement has no head, but it does have a center: the Institute for Policy Studies, a Washington, D.C. research organization. IPS serves as a source of funds, and a clearing-house of ideas, for a network of organizations across the country; it numbers many well-known academics among its friends and Fellows; it boasts frequent contact with the more liberal members of Congress."[55]

It is doubtful that anyone from IPS would give credence to anything printed in *Barron's* but IPS co-founder Marcus Raskin is quoted in Paul Dickson's book, *Think Tanks,* as saying much the same thing.

Dickson wrote in 1970:

"Institute Fellows have been active in virtually every issue of concern to young activists. Raskin claims, 'The Institute has had a profound effect on the Movement. It's hard to pin down where our influences can really be felt, but our existence has mattered.' He explains that one way in which the Institute counts is that it is not only chronicling what is wrong but is also attempting through social experimentation to give young activists some possible answers to the question that is often asked of them: What do you propose to erect in the place of the institutions of present society?"[56]

What Raskin proposes to erect in place of the institutions of the present society is the fulfillment of a dream he and his colleagues of the Students for a Democratic Society set forth in 1966 in the prospectus of the "Radical Education Project":

"Democratic radicalism . . . the creation of a new left in America . . . deeply rooted in the traditions of utopian and scientific socialism, popular democracy and humanism . . ."[57]

The "social experimentation" Raskin mentioned is now being devised by the IPS staff in the form of policy papers and legislative proposals submitted to friendly legislators at the federal, state and local levels.

IPS was founded in 1963 by Raskin and Richard J. Barnet. Having met in April, 1961 at a joint White House and State Department conference on disarmament, they discovered they had a common "contempt and hostility toward the whole military-industrial establishment sitting there at one table," and decided to do something about it. Raskin was at that time an aide to McGeorge Bundy within the staff of the National Security Council. He had come to Washington in 1959 as an aide in a Wisconsin congressman's office, and then had become a consultant to a group of twelve congressmen. Barnet had degrees from Harvard Law School and Princeton's Center for International Studies. He had become a consultant to the Departments of Defense and State. When he and Raskin met, he was Deputy Director for Political Research of the U.S. Arms Control and Disarmament Agency. He had just turned 32, and only days before meeting Raskin, had received his GS-15 appointment to the Disarmament agency. The two of them continued to work in government as they put IPS together. Raskin was a member of the U.S. delegation to the Geneva talks on disarmament in 1962 and in the period between 1963, when IPS was formally opened, and 1965, he was an education advisor to the Bureau of the Budget, a member of the Presidential Panel on Educational Research and Development, and a consultant to the White House Office of Science and Technology. It was only in 1965 that he dropped all affiliations with the federal government because of his objection to the Vietnam War and what he termed "the militarization of universities."

His timing seems to have been propitious. Four IPS Fellows were among those arrested in New York in March of 1965, participating in what Sale described as "SDS's first official civil disobedience"—an arms-locked-together blocking of the sidewalk and doorway at the entrance to the Chase Manhattan Bank, protesting bank loans to South Africa. In January, 1968, Raskin himself was indicted, along with Dr. Benjamin Spock and three other noted activists, for conspiracy in "counseling, aiding and abetting" young men to avoid or resist the draft. It was a busy time at IPS. In 1977, looking back to his own role as an IPS Fellow in 1968, *Village Voice* staff writer Paul Cowan described his service:

> ". . . among brave, brilliant people who have theorized together, faced jail and even death together for more than a decade . . . at the Institute for Policy Studies (IPS) which has served as an intellectual headquarters for the left since 1962 . . . We didn't just talk, though— we planned. Demonstrations at the Democratic Convention in Chicago. Ways of preventing police brutality toward blacks. Draft resistance. The formation of communes. Politics was like a religion in 1968, and it seemed to unify all our action . . ."[58]

Raskin and Barnet had formed a nucleus of bright and energetic people. Some of them were committed radicals including some vintage SDSers, but they had also brought onto their board an impressive representation of people with respected liberal, rather than radical, credentials. They began with moderate forms of activism. They held seminars, and invited congressmen and other government officials as participants. In mid-1978, they were maintaining a highly visible respectability as consultants for various congressmen. They claimed, in the pages of *Mother Jones,* to have been asked by fifty-four members of Congress to analyze the federal budget. They published that analysis, and included the names of the congressmen.

For a long time, they had cultivated these fifty-four legislators among others in key positions. They had recruited, as an IPS Fellow, Richard F. Kaufman, staff director of the Joint Congressional Economic Committee. According to Paul Dickson, Kaufman continued to function in both roles:

> "In his [Kaufman's] role as an Institute Fellow he has been involved in a project called the Congressional Seminar on Military Procurement, which ran from 1968 through 1970. It began when Kaufman contacted congressional offices asking to speak to whoever works on military spending and then, after getting to speak to the man in charge, asking him if he would be interested in meeting on the subject of

improper procurement practices, defense spending, and its influence on the economy and the need for reform. His calls netted 35 congressional aides who met in regular seminars over the two-year period. At its conclusion, the nucleus of those who had attended the seminar formed an informal congressional Review Committee to keep an eye on defense spending. Such seminars are not uncommon at the Institute [IPS], with gatherings being held for such groups as Members of Congress for Peace Through Law, the Council for a Livable World, and the Mobilization Committee to End the War."[59]

Dickson notes in another place within the fourteen pages he devoted to IPS in his book that the organization did not "sit too well with many elements of official Washington." He cites two examinations by IRS to see if its activities could be construed as lobbying—especially after Raskin's indictment in the antidraft case. Senator Strom Thurmond is quoted as saying in 1967:

"By giving a tax exemption to an organization like the Institute for Policy Studies, our government is allowing tax exemption to support revolution."[60]

Dickson adds that on the floor of the Senate in 1969, Sen. Thurmond characterized IPS as an "elite" trying to make changes without reference to the desires of the American people, and he singled out the Institute's participation in "the recent attack on the Administration's military procurement authorization bill."

Senator Paul Fannin of Arizona is described as another who "fumed" against IPS. Dickson says when he learned that IPS's Arthur Waskow was being used as a consultant to American University's Center for the Administration of Justice—which had a grant from the Justice Department—he said:

"Personally, I think that we can bear an investigation into the circumstances that allow U. S. taxpayers' money to be used in payment of consultant fees to a man who had led demonstrations demanding community control of the police . . ."[61]

But, Dickson continues, IPS has refused to be rattled by its critics:

". . . though not eager to lose its tax privileges, Raskin vows, 'I can't imagine that there is any kind of pressure that will cause the Institute to roll over and die.' One of the main reasons for such fortitude, in his view, is the character of its Fellows, to whom he ascribes the collective qualities of '. . . brilliance, integrity and bravery.' As for the Institute's detractors, Raskin says: 'We refuse to take them too seriously because if we were responsible for all of the things they claim we are, then we would be the most important institution in America.' "[62]

Although that comment was intended as ironic, it may well have reflected the aspirations of the speaker, for, at that time, in early 1969, IPS was launching two satellite institutes—the Cambridge Institute in Massachusetts and the Bay Area Institute in California. One major project in Cambridge was an attempt to "uncover ways in which urban working-class families can more actively participate in American social and political life and effect social change."[63] Out of such projects have come radical organizing activities at the proverbial "grassroots." The Bay Area Institute was designed to document "ecological perils" and to "offer plans for dealing with them," and to investigate "the force of capital, technology and the tools of war in the Pacific."

In June, 1970 IPS launched the Institute for Southern Studies in Atlanta, co-directed by Georgia State Senator Julian Bond and IPS Fellow Sue Thrasher—with Dr. Peter Bourne soon coming onto the advisory board. Its initial programs included an examination of the impact of defense spending on the South, a study of the black movement, critiques of regional poverty programs and "an oral-history project aimed at filling in the gaps in the history books by presenting the histories of Southern people such as the East Kentucky coal miner."[64]

Back at headquarters, IPS personnel were busy infiltrating a number of Washington projects. One was the Institute for Self-Reliance, a vehicle for advancing IPS theories about what might be called "decentralized collectivism." Another was the National Conference for Alternative State and Local Public Policies, headed up by a former "old guard" SDSer who had done a stint as the Washington bureau chief for the openly Marxist-Leninist newspaper, *Guardian*. The NCASLPP maintains communications with, and holds annual gatherings for, radicals occupying public office and other IPS sympathizers interested in state and local government. Prominent among the participants have been: Paul Soglin, mayor of Madison, Wisconsin; Sam Brown, Colorado state treasurer and now head of ACTION; and Justin Ravitz, the professed Marxist lawyer elected as a criminal court judge in Detroit. Another major activity which operates under the main office of IPS is the Government Accountability Project which seeks to locate and encourage possible sources of information for "whistle-blowing" activity within the government. IPS has had a hand in the Middle East Research and Information Project, which supports guerrilla activities in that area of the world. It has also been involved in the establishment of the Center for National Security Studies, an activity operating primarily against U. S. foreign and domestic intelligence-gathering capabilities. IPS personnel have been supportive of several other antidefense and anti-intelligence gathering organizations in Washington. Raskin himself became a member of the advisory board of the radical group that began the publication of *Counterspy,* known for its publicizing of U.S. CIA agents—one of whom was shot to death in Greece shortly after his name had appeared in the magazine. IPS Fellow Michael Klare has been involved in the antinuclear-power coalition, Mobilization for Survival. Indeed he is one of its task force leaders.

As IPS has grown stronger, it has become increasingly radical, even to the point of enrolling as Fellows known revolutionaries and terrorists. Nowhere has this been more obvious than in its international endeavors, especially in its formation of the Transnational Institute with a full-fledged branch in Amsterdam, as well as a substantial operation in London. Tariq Ali is one of the better known extremists to come into IPS through its Transnational Institute. Richard Neville, himself an underground newspaper editor and sometime fugitive from British law, wrote of the three "Marx brothers: Danny, Rudi and Tariq" (European revolutionaries Danny Cohn-Bendit and "Red Rudi" Dutschke, and Pakistani revolutionary Tariq Ali).[65] Georgia Congressman Larry MacDonald described Tariq Ali in the Congressional Record as leader of the British section of the Trotskyite "Fourth International" and active in the international effort to provide manpower and support to Sao Eirie, a practicing terrorist organization in England and Ireland. J. B. Hutton's book, *The Subversives,*[66] describes his labor agitation at a Ford plant in England, when Ali was editor of the underground paper, *Black Dwarf,* and on the editorial board of another underground, *Red Mole.* In his detailed volume, *Terrorism,* Walter Laqueur cites Ali's membership on the executive board of the Fourth International, and links his name with that of Ernest Mandel — Belgian revolutionary Marxist and one of the founders of the West German SDS — as a fellow advocate of terrorism.[67] David Kelley suggests Ali and his Trotskyite international organization maintain contacts with terrorist groups worldwide, and reports Argentine police allegations that they have received ransom money from a kidnapping in that country.[68] Ali himself, in response to a Canadian TV reporter's question about the use of political violence, said: "I would say that this is largely a tactical question, depending precisely on the degree of opposition we encounter in our struggle for socialism."

Another IPS figure of international notoriety was Orlando Letelier, a former cabinet-level official in the overthrown Marxist government of Chile. Soon after he came to the U. S. as an exile in 1975, he became first an IPS Fellow and then director of its Transnational Institute. On September 21, 1976, he and a young woman associate were killed in a bombing as they drove along the streets of Washington. After the initial shock of the bombing subsided, stories began to surface in the press about mysterious papers Letelier had had in a briefcase in his car when it was bombed. There was great secrecy about these papers, first on the part of the police who seized them initially, then on the part of the IPS personnel into whose custody they were given after police and

FBI examination. However, several newsmen, including columnists Evans and Novak and Jack Anderson, and *Washington Star* writer, Jeremiah O'Leary, gained access to them at some point. They reported in their columns and news stories that Letelier was in contact not only with a number of important members of Congress in Washington but had considerable dealings with individuals, institutions and government officials in Cuba, East Germany and the Soviet Union, and that he had been collecting $1,000 through a "Havana connection" for mysterious work he was undertaking. Jack Anderson even reported contacts between Letelier and "the Cuban planning group that directs the subversion of Puerto Rico and the United States." As director of the IPS/Transnational Institute, Letelier had a convenient base for whatever may have been his mission.

The most often quoted passage in the published commentary about IPS appears in the introduction Paul Dickson wrote to the fourteen pages he devoted to this organization in his book *Think Tanks.* Dickson, whose articles have appeared in such vehicles as *Esquire, Saturday Review, Nation,* the *Washington Monthly,* the *Washington Post* and the *Progressive,* begins the section on IPS with: "Washington's Institute for Policy Studies, the farthest one can travel to the Left on the think-tank continuum." Then he writes:

> "The Institute for Policy Studies is attempting to lay the groundwork for the new society that will replace the present collapsing one. It not only has dedicated itself to ushering in the new society by inquiry and experimentation but is also doing what it can to hasten the demise of the present one."[69]

As noted above, David Kelley in *Barron's* asserted that IPS is the "center of the movement." It is, in fact, the switchyard of communications and traffic moving to deliver on the "anti-Establishment--and-generally-to-the-left-of-political-center" philosophy which, as the *Los Angeles Times* and *New Yorker* articles stated, animates the alternative media. Among the personnel and adherents of IPS are to be found a variety of positions to the left of political center. At one end are liberal-minded people with no clearly definable political ideology. Indeed, they seem not to give much conscious thought to such matters, but move among political leftists in order to advance cultural permissiveness or disarmament or some other goal. At the other end of this spectrum are people whose calculated political objectives are so far to the left that their dreams cannot be realized in any recognizable version of the present system, but can only be achieved through "social reconstruction" toward the model of Cuba, East Germany, the Soviet Union or the Allende regime in Chile.

The IPS has been allotted extensive space in this analysis because the breadth of philosophical commitment it embraces, combined with the power and momentum it has generated, place it at the pinnacle of influence upon the alternative media. This is an influence which has been growing for some time. Robert Glessing states in *The Underground Press in America* that the first underground paper to appear in the nation's capital, the *Washington Free Press,* was founded by "students at the Washington, D. C. Institute of Policy Studies."[70] This publication lasted about three years. When it ceased publishing, some of its staff went to the new underground paper that had just been started, *Quicksilver Times,* some went eventually to the *Guardian* in New York, and some made their way to Liberation News Service. IPS people were in and out of the offices, and pages of *Quicksilver Times* during the three years of its existence. Subsequently a new underground paper, *Colonial Times,* was started in Washington. It had even greater IPS involvement. When that died, its key staff members were instrumental in starting *Newsworks.* One IPS staff member moved from *Colonial Times* to *Newsworks* and finally to a top editorial position at *Mother Jones* in California.

IPS has always had prolific writers, a number of whom have written for the more liberal large metropolitan newspapers as well as for the underground and alternative press. Their articles appear in literary, religious and sex magazines. One of its associates, Jeremy Rifkin, of PBC, had articles published in *Saturday Review* and the flesh-peddling *Gallery* almost simultaneously. Other IPS authors appear in radical religious publications such as the *Other Side* and the *Witness.* The IPS satellites have produced their own publications. One of long standing is *Southern Exposure,* published by the IPS Institute for Southern Studies; *Working Papers for a New Society* emerged from the IPS offshoot in Cambridge; and the *Elements* is published by the Transnational Institute. *Working Papers* illustrates Paul Dickson's comment, advocating alternatives to the institutions of society and doing what it can to hasten the demise of existing ones. *Mother Jones* is a product of the IPS Bay Area Institute's activities. Its masthead always states that the magazine is published by the "Foundation for National Progress" and within both editorial and advertising texts, it points to that Foundation as its "parent organization." On occasion, however, it speaks of "The Institute for Policy Studies, our parent organization." The latter attribution occurs, for instance, when *Mother Jones* provides information about the annual National Conference of Alternative State and Local Public Policies. At other times, it may refer to IPS and the Foundation for National Progress as if they are two unrelated organizations. Articles by IPS personnel are common features in *Mother Jones.*

IPS has apparently provided "seed money" to launch its satellite organizations and their publications, and then granted them a sort of franchise status with responsibility for raising their own money. In a *Village Voice* article, former IPS Fellow Paul Cowan wrote that the organization raised about $14 million in its first decade. The money came from wealthy individuals who were sympathetic to IPS goals, and from foundations—Ford, the Stern Family Fund, the National Board of Missions of the Presbyterian Church, the Field Foundation and the Milbank Foundations, according to Dickson's *Think Tanks.*[71]

In a Heritage Foundation publication of May, 1977 entitled "Institute for Policy Studies," the Stern Family Fund is cited as a source, as is the Ford Foundation and the National Board of Missions of the Presbyterian Church, the Bernstein Foundation, the Fontaney Corporation, the Janss Foundation, the Rubin Foundation, the San Francisco Foundation, the Sperry family, the Warburg family.[72]

The Alternatives Among Workers

In our listing of politically oriented alternative media, there are some that are concentrated in the field of labor: the *New Unionist Newsletter* of Minneapolis; *Peoples World,* Berkeley; *Root & Branch,* Cambridge, Mass.; *Spark,* Detroit; and the *Worker,* published in both Seattle, Washington and Portland, Oregon. With the exception of *People's World,* which is an old publication, this is a family of periodicals founded by the "New Left." Various publications for workers have arisen in conjunction with a specific strike or organizing campaign, only to disappear at the conclusion of the action, and in some cases, to be revived later.

In recent years, union officials have been as surprised and distressed as company managers about wildcat strikes and/or militant radicalism that have occurred in the ranks of organized labor. Quite often such action has been precipitated by the appearance of a publication intended as an *alternative* to the established union publications. Almost every union sponsors some type of publication. Most of them, while being aggressively prolabor and determined to drive a hard bargain in behalf of the members, are not committed to destroying the prevailing economic system. The radicalism that surfaces here and there is encouraged, if not directly coordinated, by the alternative media in general, and worker-oriented alternatives in particular. It is significant that regular union publications are not found in the directories of alternative publications, whereas the radical publications aimed at the workers are.

When a story appears in the daily press quoting the complaints of union officials about "the communists" providing support for an unauthorized strike or violence in a plant, they are usually not referring to anyone from the "Old Left" Communist Party of the U.S.A. They are talking about militants from a variety of "New Left"-extremist formations, most often one of the Maoist or Trotskyite groups. The old-time far-leftists are fairly well known and follow generally recognized patterns in their activities. The new militants are not well known nor do they have any standard practices. They are following the call to "go out and organize among the workers." Among the busier organizations in this respect are two "New Left" groups that grew out of the disintegrated SDS. They are the former October League, now calling itself the Communist Party (Marxist-Leninist) or CP-ML and the Revolutionary Union, now calling itself the Revolutionary Communist Party, or RCP. Both have been active and disruptive in labor relationships with management.

A recent illustration of this phenomenon occurred in a wildcat strike against the new Volkswagen plant in Pennsylvania, of special concern because it indicates the interest of the general alternative publications in labor unrest and the clashes that may occur between their efforts and those of the more action-oriented alternatives. In this incident, two staff members from *In These Times* drove to the site of the plant at New Stanton, 35 miles southeast of Pittsburgh. Local union officials and members were trying to handle an unauthorized strike then in its fourth day. As the two writers approached the picket lines, they had an encounter which was reported later in their paper, as follows:

" 'Who are you affiliated with?'

'Hi,' I answered, extending a copy of *In These Times*. 'We're here to do a story for *In These Times*, a national newspaper coming out of Chicago.'

'That's a godamn Communist newspaper and we don't want you here,' the leader stated. A grim looking clump of men now surrounded us.

'It's not a Communist newspaper,' I answered. 'The most it might be accused of is being a socialist newspaper. Have you ever seen a copy?'

'I don't need to. It's a damn Communist newspaper and we don't want you here. We ought to take your damn newspapers and burn them in the trash can over there. Now, if you know what's good for you, you'll get your ass out of here, fast!'

'We just want to ask a few questions . . .'

'And we're not answering. You can go ask your damn questions in Russia where you came from. You're just causing trouble here, where you don't belong,' the leader continued, poking his finger into my chest. 'Now leave before we do some damage to you.' "

The two writers left that gate and tried to approach the plant at another point, but were again blocked and not even allowed to get out of their car. Finally, amid threats that if they did not drive on, they would have their kneecaps broken, a leaflet was shoved in their car window: "Here, take this with you. Your pals left it!" Looking at the mimeographed paper as they drove away, they still could not decide what about it upset the men so. They quickly saw, however, where it had come from. The logo at the top of the paper read: "NUWO." They looked at each other, "National United Workers Organization. That's a front group of the Revolutionary Communist Party — the communists the men were so angry about!" [73]

One interesting aspect of this incident is the presumed difference in viewpoints. The two writers had identified the Revolutionary Communist Party as the problem, and seemed to suppose that if the organization had not been at the plant first, their own paper would have been welcome. This may or may not have been true. If, however, a copy of *In These Times* is compared to the *Worker*, which is one of several published by the Revolutionary Communist Party, and *Peoples World*, which is an "Old Left" Communist labor paper, it is difficult to discern the distinction the two reporters seemed to feel should be apparent. The difference in interpretation of revolutionary dogma is apparent only to the sophisticated reader.

The Overtly Marxist Alternatives

Marxism is certainly not absent from many of the publications already touched upon. However, the ones now to be considered seem to have chosen the exploration or elaboration of Marxism as a primary objective.

The newest among these is *Marxist Perspectives,* conceived and planned over the past two to three years by a group of Marxist scholars who asserted they did not have a sympathetic place to publish their writings. Under the editorship of Eugene D. Genovese, professor of history at the University of Rochester, and with an editorial board composed of faculty members from an impressive list of colleges and universities across the country, Eugene Genovese and his publisher, Warren Susman of Rutgers, are listed on the masthead of *In These*

Times as "sponsors" of that paper. Conversely, the co-publishers of *In These Times*, James Weinstein and William Sennett, joined with nearly two dozen of their sponsors and associates in lending their names to the promotional literature of *Marxist Perspectives*. This promotional material promises the magazine will be "free of factional polemics" and will publish discussions of practical applications of Marxism to a wide variety of subjects: science and art, psychology and sociology, economics and politics, law and manners. It is too early to judge the success or impact, but *U. S. News & World Report* mentioned a ready market for it because of the increased spread of Marxist ideas on U. S. campuses, and the elevation of Marxist-oriented scholars to positions of importance in such organizations as the American Economic Association, the American Political Science Association and the Organization of American Historians. [74]

Monthly Review is a 64-page magazine started in 1949 by the late Leo Huberman and Paul Sweezy, both of whom were close to the student upheaval and SDS. In his book, *The New Left Today,* Phillip Abbott Luce says it was they who convinced young American militants that Castro and his government were not communist. The magazine covers "imperialism" and "liberation movements" all over the world, has a Spanish edition and for a while had an Italian edition. It is mentioned by *Source Catalogue* as the "patriarch of U.S. Marxist" publications. It uses a "Marxist-Leninist approach in its analyses of economic, social and political problems and advocates socialism [or communism] as an economic system to replace capitalism." Its circulation is probably around 10,000 and it runs a monthly program on a New York listener-supported radio station.

News & Letters is a tabloid size paper published in Detroit to advance the philosophy of Marxist humanism.

Radical America, now published from Cambridge, Massachusetts, was started in 1967 in Madison, Wisconsin as an "SDS Journal of American Radicalism," according to Muller and Spahn in *From Radical Left to Extreme Right.* It is commended by *In These Times* and, in fact, shares some sponsors with that publication. It claims to be "an independent socialist and feminist journal" now "entering its second decade of publication." Its topical emphasis is upon organizing activities, especially directed to people concerned with "the working class," "racism," "sexism," and "socialist strategy." The following excerpt from its July-August 1972 edition illustrates its views on feminism:

> "Marx did not fail to recognize that the specific task of the proletarian revolution was to remove the mantle of slavery from the woman in her role of wife and mother. Indeed, he went so far in the *1844 Manuscripts* as to measure the progress of humanity by the relations between the sexes . . . In our own century, the convergence of woman's

increasing social strength and the step-by-step disintegration of the family has produced a glaring contradiction between actual power and accepted standards. With the decay of the older values, an accumulating weight falls upon all women, and potentials for understanding and activity denied since the dawn of industrialization are irrevocably released. (4)"[75]

There is little general understanding of how much the alternative media depend on achieving their aims through changes in the cultural institutions, not just in the political and economic spheres. The (4) above refers to a footnote which states:

"(4) So clearly has this permeated popular consciousness that a notable woman journalist can speak of 'a breakthrough in human sexuality . . . [which] is going to occur because women will start taking charge of their own sex lives.' Barbara Seaman: 'The Liberated Orgasm' in *Ms.*, August 1972. Even granted the loose usage of the term 'revolution' by such magazines as *Ms.*, there is a serious expectation that we are on the threshold of a change in relations which will transform the most intimate aspects of human life, and thereby (whether *Ms.* considers this point or not) the entirety of human life."[76]

Here is an illustration of the views of the alternative press being promoted by *Ms.*, a publication that many consider to be a part of the "Establishment," and being criticized for its loose usage of revolution. The *Ms.* passage thus disparaged was:

"I think it's so wonderful that women have discovered masturbation, because it will enable us to keep apart from men as long as necessary. When you have work to do, you can't allow yourself to be diverted by sexual relationships. Masturbation is what male revolutionaries have always done to relieve themselves."[77]

Should there be surprise at the Marxist interest in *Ms.* or *Ms.'s* countercultural and militant tones, it should be noted that the magazine was not always so subtle about its phraseology.[78]

Socialist Review is described by *Resources Catalogue* as having a "Heavy Marxist-Leninist perspective." In other words, it deals not just in Marxism as an "analytical tool" as appears to be the intention of the scholars who initiated *Marxist Perspectives,* but in the promulgation of "the struggle for communism" which was Lenin's interest in the matter. The catalogue's annotation is significant in that it is published by a collective with a Marxist-Leninist orientation. A perusal of *Socialist Review* confirms the catalogue's assessment. This, incidentally, is the publication mentioned earlier as having been founded under the name *Socialist Revolution* by James Weinstein, who subsequently founded and now is co-publisher of *In These Times.*

Workforce is a quarterly variation of the *Resources Catalogue,* one of the five directories consulted for this study. Both are published by Vocations for Social Change, Inc., of Oakland, California, which sometimes speaks of itself as "a tax-exempt antiprofit corporation/ collective" and includes a copyright statement with the qualifier: "movement groups may use the contents freely!" As another illustration of interrelationships among alternative media, the catalogue edition at hand, dated January 1978, gives credit in its masthead for help received from *Southern Exposure,* the magazine published by the Atlanta-based Institute for Southern Studies, itself an offspring of the Institute for Policy Studies of Washington, D.C. Earlier it was noted that one of the members of the editorial board of *Mother Jones* was formerly a representative for Vocations for Social Change at Berkeley. The idea for the organization seems to have come out of the Students for a Democratic Society. In his book *The Riot Makers,* Eugene Methvin wrote:

> "SDS headquarters devised a catalog of 'Vocations for Radicals' listing scores of leftist operations offering jobs, including even radical community action agencies financed by the federal Office of Economic Opportunity. The ultimate is to have hundreds of nonprofit enterprises—bookstores, newspapers, record shops, radio stations, poster manufacturers, printshops and sales outlets—in dozens of communities, supporting two or three people each, in full-time propaganda and organizational warfare, climatizing America for disruption."[79]

The idea was enlarged. The catalogue of activities would not be as limited as Methvin's description indicates. The listings would include cultural as well as political and economic entries. A table of contents would typically read:

Aging	Health
Back to the Land Lifestyles	Housing
Birth	Jobs and Careers
Children	Labor
Communities	Law
Cultural Arts	Media
Distribution	Native Americans
Ecology	Peace and Draft
Education	Prisons and Prisoners
Energy Alternatives	Resource Guides
Environmental Organizing	Small Press
Food	Social, Political and
Gay	Economic Change

Spirituality/Consciousness   Women
Third World   Miscellaneous

The name was changed from one that suggested the concern was only with vocations wherein radicals could be radicals, to a name indicating concern with *vocations* that will produce *social change*—whether the people who function in them are radicals or not. Published quarterly, the catalogues became a running job mart, designed to attract talent and energy to activities culturally and politically compatible with VSC's concept of an ideal society. From the political entries and the slogans prominently featured through the text, it appears to have modeled itself after publications from Cuba, China or one of the "national liberation" regimes in the Third World. One of the requirements for a group or program to be listed is that it "must be actively involved in working for social change, not a service."

As SDS fell apart in 1969-70, the factions within its ranks scrambled for the "gold" the organization was leaving scattered across the land in the more than 350 local chapters (with a total of up to 100,000 members) throughout the country. The explosive final national convention cost SDS many of the 100,000 members but there were at least a few people in almost every chapter willing to stay and work with *something*. VSC kept its headquarters in California, but it franchised its concept out of some of these willing hands. In so doing, it provided itself with a network of communications, stopping places for its own members as they traveled about the country, and replicas of its nationally oriented publication to serve regional and local clienteles. Through such contacts it became possible to publish in its catalogues specific local services and activities such as:

> "Houston, Texas: VSC . . . a living/working collective putting out a weekly opposition newspaper; they also operate a small bookstore and are working on various publishing projects including a *people's yellow pages;* a counseling program has been started, soon to be augmented with workshops."

Emphasis was added in the above to note that the research for this study has revealed some form of "people's yellow pages" published in 38 cities and towns, most not evidencing much radicalism but selectively promoting social and cultural change much in the spirit of VSC's stated goal.

> "Bellingham, Washington: New Vocation, Fairhaven College . . . doing one-to-one counseling; involved in community cooperatives (food, alternative newspaper); will be publishing Puget Sound alternatives directory in March; have resources of alternatives all over Bellingham

and U.S."

"Ithaca, New York: VSC . . . a new working collective of nine people has just been formed and are hard at work on an Ithaca Area People's Yellow Pages. They are also starting to pull together literature for a people's reading room and are working 'on getting files and our heads together for counseling.' They are looking for a permanent location in downtown Ithaca and hope to relate to high school and community people as well as college students."

"Washington, D.C.: VSC, c/o Washington WRL [War Resisters League] at American University . . . acting as a drop-in center but going beyond simple job counseling into radical critiques of America and the need for revolutionary action; has ties with Job Coop (a place to get regular jobs) is trying to establish a community fund, develop outreach for job raps, and do local radio shows; have begun a local VSC programs' newsletter, *Workforce Counselor,* in an effort to improve communication between projects and generate new ones."

The main purpose of the catalogues is to encourage people in all parts of the country to find work through which they can promote and produce "social change." The antibusiness bias is a leitmotif. VSC catalogues always include such entries as these:

"CORPORATE INTELLIGENCE ALLIANCE, 555 W. Belden St., Chicago . . . puts out a packet of information on Chicago area corporations engaged in war-oriented research and production, including ideas for using the information."

"CORPORATE INFORMATION CENTER, National Council of Churches, 475 Riverside Dr., New York, N.Y. . . . provides research for education and action on the social impact of U.S. corporations, especially vis-à-vis the investment practices of church investors. They study the impact on the environment, consumerism, foreign investment (esp. South Africa), labor and minority practices, and military procurement. They publish Center *Briefs,* dealing with specific case studies, and the monthly *Corporate Examiner,* a digest of news and information on corporate responsibility."

"LSM [Liberation Support Movement] INFORMATION CENTER, P.O. Box 2077, Oakland, CA . . . The LSM is a radical, nonprofit political organization whose prime aim is to contribute to the *anti-imperialist and international socialist* struggle through *research, publications and educational work,* combined with various forms of *concrete support activities.* Their efforts [since 1968] have been focused primarily, though by no means exclusively, on the liberation movements of southern Africa. LSM publications [the primary one of which is *LSM News,* a quarterly magazine] include interviews with and autobiographies of southern African militants. Yearly

subscriptions . . . are $3 each. Besides their publication, LSM conducts informational tours covering much of the U.S. and Canada. This has enabled them to contact thousands of interested people with audio-visual programs. Please write for more information on material support work, film tours and complete catalogue of LSM publications."

Emphasis was added to call attention to the standard Marxist-Leninist vocabulary used here, indicating that LSM is engaged in propaganda work and material support for communist activity in other countries. Study of its literature supports that supposition.

"MIDDLE EAST RESEARCH AND INFORMATION PROJECT, Box 48, Harvard Square Station, Cambridge, MA . . . is a collective which, through its publications and educational programs, attempts to focus on the political economy of the Middle East, the U.S. role in the area and the class and national struggles of the people. They publish a monthly bulletin, *MERIP Reports,* and distribute other books and pamphlets. They also have speakers available and a slide show on the People's Democratic Republic of Yemen. For more information, write to the above address, or MERIP, Box 3122, Columbia Heights Station, Washington, D.C."

"NORTH AMERICAN CONGRESS ON LATIN AMERICA (NACLA), Box 57, Cathedral Park Station, New York City, or Box 226, Berkeley, CA 94701 . . . is a well-established research center which specializes in this country's involvement in Latin America, as well as other aspects of the military-industrial complex. Among the literature they distribute is a monthly newsletter, *NACLA's Latin America and Empire Report.* Write for a complete literature list."[80]

Party Newspapers

The alternative directories naturally do not list the Democratic and Republican Parties. Indeed, only two of our five directories listed the Communist Party of the U.S.A. and its main newspaper, the *Daily World.* It has generally been true that the alternative/underground media treat the CPUSA much as Kirkpatrick Sale describes the SDS position toward it: "The Communist Party itself was seen as a joke, a tired collection of middle-aged irrelevants who hadn't any idea of what the New Left was all about and certainly no means of taking it over."[81] In another place, Sale wrote: "Communist Party members, of whom there were no more than forty or fifty in SDS, were in many cases known to the SDS leaders anyway, though they tended to keep their affiliations from the rank and file . . . Communist infiltration was still regarded largely as a joke. The suggestion that Bettina Aptheker, Berkeley activist and CP member, had put forth at Clear Lake that the Communist Party was the logical force to lead the New Left was dismissed out of hand . . . assigning it to the dust bin."[82] Sale offers additional disparagement in reporting that in 1969 when SDS destroyed itself, one of the prime candidates available to assume the leadership was another organization that "could never shake off its Old Left heritage and its rather stuffy brand of Marxism"—the Young Socialist Alliance (YSA), youth arm of the Socialist Workers Party (SWP), which is the largest of the Trotskyite communist formations in the United States. Nevertheless, YSA/SWP did make significant gains after the breakup of SDS. Sale writes that YSA fared the best of those standing around waiting to pick up the spoils, adding: ". . . in December, for example, fifteen former SDS chapter heads announced they were joining the YSA to escape SDS's 'personality cliques.' "[83]

The belittling of the older communist organizations was undoubtedly a tactic used by the "New Left" to improve their own recruiting capacity, but these older organizations have continued to exert a strong influence in various ways. In his 750-page, 1978-published book, *Out Now!*, SWP's chief organizer, Fred Halstead, has identified the Communist Party U.S.A. and the Socialist Workers Party as prime forces in the antiwar movement, in one moment competing with each other, in the next cooperating to guide this activity in mutually beneficial directions. The main difference in the method of operation of the two parties is that the CPUSA uses a large number of organizations not openly identified as its own, or under its influence, to promote its objectives, while the SWP is more likely to work to dominate a situation overtly. The CPUSA has been remarkably successful in getting one or two of its own people into key positions in organizations on which it has no other claim. A current example of this tactic is found in the antinuclear-power group known as the Mobilization for Survival which publishes *The Mobilizer* newsletter. This publication lists as the leader of its task force on labor CPUSA National Committee member Gil Green.

The two organizations differ in the brand of communism they espouse. The CPUSA invariably supports the Soviet Union. The *Daily World* has thus denounced President Carter's human rights policies. It has called the President's Cabinet nominees captives of big business. It was particularly critical of then-Attorney General Bell, labeling him a segregationist. It called for the firing of Budget Director Bert Lance. It portrayed the fuel shortage as created by industry as a means of justifying price increases, and urged nationalization of oil as the only solution. It has continuously insisted that minorities are mistreated in the U.S., and advocated affirmative action as necessary to make up for centuries of discrimination. Allan Bakke was a special target of attack by the *Daily World.* The execution of Gary Gilmore was an occasion for renewed attacks on the death penalty as a weapon against classes traditionally suffering repression in the United States. Military spending is denounced as an obstacle to détente, especially funds going to the production of new weapons, such as the B-1 bomber, the cruise missile and the neutron bomb.

Through its party paper, the *Militant,* the SWP also attacked Bakke and advocated more affirmative action. It supports full rights for homosexuals and pushes strongly for the Equal Rights Amendment. In fact, the SWP has been denounced by the National Organization for Women for trying to exploit this issue for "socialist rather than feminist aims." The SWP response was that NOW was "red-baiting." SWP supported radical candidate Ed Sadlowski for presidency of the steelworkers' union, giving him extensive space in the *Militant.* It continuously supports "independence" for Puerto Rico, as espoused by the terrorist FALN that has claimed credit for setting off bombs in New York, Chicago and Washington. For its own part, it shies away from openly advocating terrorism. It claims to be against political violence, but it continues affiliation with the Fourth International, the Trotskyite international organization which does support terrorism. When pushed on the matter, SWP spokesmen are likely to argue that there may be times when violence is simply necessary to achieve political goals. The SWP denounces the United States more fervently than any other country, but it has sharply criticized Russia and China for their "Stalinism" and has railed against the Eurocommunists in Western Europe. It tends to support the policies of such countries as Mozambique, Vietnam and Cambodia, but denounces them for repression. There is no topic over which it has been more outspoken than "government spying," especially with regard to its own activities, and it has filed and vigorously pressed a $40 million lawsuit against the FBI.

Other party papers listed by the directories, along with their organizational publishers, are:

Black Panther—Black Panther Party
Call—Communist Party (Marxist-Leninist)
Challenge—Progressive Labor Party
Gramma—Communist Party of Cuba
Revolution—Revolutionary Communist Party
Weekly People—Socialist Labor Party
Workers Power—International Socialists
Workers Vanguard—Spartacist League
Workers World—Workers World Party

Most of the above are of relatively little importance, the sponsoring organizations having declined in their influence or never having had much influence at all. The Black Panther Party has lost membership and clout but its radical, "antisystem" tendency persists. It has simply engaged in more subtle and perhaps more effective organizing, instead of the flamboyant tactics which characterized its earlier undertakings. The Progressive Labor Party has also declined. To some extent, it was an SDS casualty with parallel internal ideological differences. *Gramma*, the Cuban Communist Party paper, was listed in only one of the directories, *Resources Catalogue*, but it was quoted and copied frequently in the old underground papers.

The Socialist Labor Party, publisher of *Weekly People*, advocates "scientific socialism" under which capitalism would be abolished and the workers would receive "the full social value of the product of their labor." It holds that Russian, Chinese and similar forms of "so-called Communism are bureaucratic state despotism that have nothing in common with Marxist Socialism." The paper was established in 1890 and has a circulation of probably no more than 15,000. The Socialist Labor Party should not be confused with the U. S. Labor Party (USLP) which publishes a widely distributed newspaper, *New Solidarity*, and three magazines, *Campaigner*, *Fusion* and *Executive Intelligence Review*. None of these was listed in the directories we used, but some information on the U.S. Labor Party might help avoid confusing it with other groups. It sometimes calls itself the "National Caucus of Labor Committees" and was formed inside a New York chapter of SDS in 1968 by the then 46-year old Lyndon Larouche. No one, either on the right or left, has come forward with a fully credible explanation of its current status or objectives. It was obviously leftist in the beginning, subsequently attacked other groups on the left—even resorting on occasion to physical violence—and eventually fell into a still-continuing pattern of overtures to the right. One of the most frequently used vehicles for this thrust has been USLP's development of a pronuclear-power stance, reflected in its *Fusion* magazine. Some groups on the right have accepted these overtures and have even entered into temporary alliances with U.S. Labor on various issues. On the other hand, some commentators on the right have suggested that U.S. Labor is still leftist, a cleverly manipulated front serving the interests of the Soviet Union. These commentators theorize that USLP's attacks on the pro-Soviet Communist Party U.S.A. could well be a manipulative cloak for the organization's true objectives. There seems to be no documentation of this view, but an examination of several editions of *Fusion* reveals it to give a significant amount of attention to the interests of East Germany and the Soviet Union.

Workers Power is published by the International Socialists, headquartered in Detroit. The organization is a splinter from the American Socialist Party that now has "local committees" in perhaps a dozen cities. Their literature describes "I.S." as being part of the "international struggle for socialism," aimed at the destruction of capitalism and the building of a "classless society." This organization had some involvement with SDS and the antiwar movement.

The Spartacist League is a splinter from the Socialist Workers Party, as is the Workers World Party. In the book *Left of Liberal*, Anthony Bouscaren and Daniel Lyons point out that there has been considerable splintering from the SWP:

> "Factionalism in the Socialist Workers Party has been responsible for the formation of other subversive groups which follow the teachings of Trotsky but differ over the means by which the goal of worldwide Communism is to be attained. Johnson-Forest Group, the Workers World Party, the Workers League (formerly known as the American Committee for the Fourth International), and the revolutionary Committee of the Fourth International, also known as the Spartacist League."[84]

Two publications among these party papers deserve special attention—the *Call* and *Revolution*—both published by organizations that openly support Maoism. The organizations claiming allegiance to Mao disagree with each other as to what Maoism is and who are Mao's true disciples in the United States. The upheavals in China following Mao's death intensified these disagreements and caused extended arguments between the two largest Maoist factions: the Revolutionary Communist Party (RCP) and the Communist Party (Marxist-Leninist) or "CP(ML)."[85]

Both the RCP and the CP(ML) prospered from the destruction of SDS. The CP(ML) was actually founded out of the SDS ruins. It began in late 1969 as the "October League" under the chairmanship of Michael Klonsky, immediate past national secretary of SDS and son of a long-time CPUSA organizer. In June, 1977 it held a "founding congress" at which it dropped its old name and established itself under the new one. In July, 1977 Klonsky and several associates were received and publicly welcomed in Peking by Hua Kuo-Feng and other officials of the new Chinese leadership. Upon their return to the U.S., Klonsky's group began the consolidation of its gains from this distinction, taking over control of the US-China Peoples Friendship Association with chapters in almost every large American city. Following the Peking line, the CP(ML) regularly denounces both superpowers but contends that since the United States has fallen behind Soviet Russia militarily, the Russians are the bigger threat. It also denounces the CPUSA as the most dangerous of the "bourgeois parties" in the United States. It has always been active in trying to organize radical caucuses in labor unions and has recently given special emphasis to the black cause. It has worked to establish small representations in large industrial areas, and is concentrating now in the South, which has been especially resistant to the socialist efforts to organize the workers. A recent example is its coverage of a racial disturbance in Tupelo, Mississippi. The CP(ML)'s national newspaper, the *Call*, suddenly appeared with inch-high headlines reading: "TUPELO: BATTLE IN THE BLACK BELT"[86] and a front-page box calling attention to the "Special Tupelo Supplement" inside. The contents offered very little about Tupelo, and the supplement was on "Black Liberation," featuring a piece by Harry Haywood, one of the 1930s authors of the "self-determination" theory.

The CP(ML)'s predecessor in Peking's favor, the RCP (Revolutionary Communist Party) was founded in 1968 in San Francisco as the Revolutionary Union. The chairman and one of its several founders was 25-year-old Robert B. Avakian, a prominent SDS organizer on the West Coast. He and others in the founding nucleus of the Revolutionary Union had been active in the SDS's Radical Revolutionary Union's first newspaper, the *Bay Area Worker*, carried the same post office box address that was listed elsewhere as that of the Bay Area Radical Education Project. The founders of the Revolutionary Union were a strange mix. In addition to those from SDS, two were in their mid-fifties and had long histories of membership in communist groups. Two had spent several years living in mainland China. Both of these had developed important contacts in China and undoubtedly used them for RU purposes.

Avakian himself was in the thick of the fight for control of SDS at the 1969 national convention in Chicago. The Revolutionary Union had been asked to bring a large group to Chicago to help fend off the takeover attempt of the Progressive Labor Party. Like most other organizations that participated in the SDS debacle, the Revolutionary Union gathered some new recruits from the SDS membership, and the opportunity to co-opt some of the local chapters. Avakian and a large group of Revolutionary Union members made a triumphant trip to Peking more than five months before President Nixon's visit. The warm reception by the Chinese leaders not only demonstrated to others on the U. S. left that China considered the Revolutionary Union to be the prime Maoist organization in the country, but set a pattern for subsequent trips by Americans who would come back to the U.S. singing the praises of the "New China" under the auspices of the US-China Peoples Friendship Association. Two ranking members of the Revolutionary Union subsequently held high offices in the US-China Peoples Friendship Association. One of these, William H. Hinton, influential in founding both RU and USCPFA, was the Friendship Association's chairman from its beginning in 1974 to 1976. His credentials as a Maoist were impressive. He had spent most of the Korean War years in the newly established People's Republic of China and had written several books on the subject. His contacts in China included his sister, Joan Hinton Engst, a nuclear physicist who defected to Peking in 1949 after having worked as a scientist at Los Alamos.

Another prominent figure in the Revolutionary Union/US-China Peoples Friendship Association was Clark Kissinger, who served in the Association variously as national vice chairman and member of the national steering committee. His credentials as a "New Leftist" were impressive. He was, at three separate times, national secretary of SDS, figured prominently in the battle that destroyed SDS, and headed up the staff of the Chicago bureau of the Maoist-oriented underground/alternative newspaper *Guardian,* before joining the Revolutionary Union.

Significant information is available on the inner workings of the Revolutionary Union because the FBI managed to get at least two informers into its ranks during its formative stages. The insight provided from this source is helpful in understanding the motives and tactics of the far left, and the alternative media. Extremist organizations are almost compulsive in their determination to put their ideas, feelings and goals into print. The first public evidence of the Revolutionary Union was a large ad in the *Black Panther.* Shortly thereafter RU leaflets were on the streets in the San Francisco area. Then a newspaper was started. Within two years, RU was operating three underground newspapers in localities not far from each other: *People Get Ready, Salt of the Earth* and *Wildcat* (later renamed the *Worker*). Today, although the national newspaper, *Revolution,* is the largest and most widely circulated of the organization's publications, RU produces local papers, newsletters or leaflets wherever it operates.

The Revolutionary Union changed its name to the Revolutionary Communist Party (RCP) in 1976 and much of the following information predates that name change. Much of this information refers to the operations of the RCP in the San Francisco area, although its headquarters have since moved to Chicago. In early 1971 the RCP began its effort to infiltrate industry. The early targets were communications and transportation services, including city and school bus operators, telephone and telegraph companies and the U.S. Postal Service. This endeavor has since reached into industries in many fields, including automobile manufacturing, as noted earlier. The strategy calls for RCP members to get jobs in a particular industry and join the union. From such positions they accuse the union leadership of being a tool of the capitalist system and seek to form a dissident caucus within the union. Sympathetic workers are recruited by RCP members for continuing discussions of complaints with the intent to foment alienation from both the union and the employer. The next step is to bring the dissident caucus under RCP control for future use in promoting strikes and advancing RCP influence throughout the union and industry. There have been failures as well as successes in this strategy, but the members are painstakingly indoctrinated and tightly disciplined. They have been quite successful in getting little knots of their people into industries in every section of the country.

The basic organizational building block of RCP is the "collective." Each collective has its own area of concern and function. It is composed of not less than three people and not more than ten. The collective is not merely a vocational affiliation for the member, it is the core of his life. It is not an instrument of control in the management sense, but a device for spreading doctrine and developing discipline in accordance with "Marxist-Leninist-Mao Tse-tung thought." This discipline includes requirements for the member to submit every aspect of his life to the will of RCP. Assurance that this submission is total and continuous is maintained by formalized criticism from other members, and self-criticism on the part of the member at weekly collective meetings. Security throughout the organization is maintained by preventing members of a collective from having access to detailed information regarding the membership or activities of other collectives, even if they may be located in the same city or geographical area.

In 1970 in the San Jose, California area, there were five RCP collectives. Two were workers collectives, two student collectives, and one was a community collective. The members belonging to a workers collective were ordered to get jobs in certain industries and then to follow the strategy outlined above. The student collectives were instructed to disseminate RCP literature to students, to see that antiwar, anticapitalist and prosocialist films were shown on campus, and to identify potential candidates for membership in RCP. They were also to take advantage of any unrest or demonstration that could be used to increase student alienation and promote a revolutionary spirit. The community collective recruited among the unemployed. It sought to work within community organizations, to form front groups, such as tenants' unions, to exploit problems of the poorer elements in the area, and to publish a newspaper. The FBI informants reported:

> "I was a member of the community collective. We had many out-reaches, like infiltrating the Welfare Rights Organization, putting out this newspaper, *Salt of the Earth*, running tenants' unions or causing them to be formed as front groups. . ."[87]

Another former member of the RCP in San Jose said he:

> ". . . became a member of the [RCP] through association with the San Jose Tenants' Union, which [he] described as having been formed in late 1969 or early 1970 by VISTA volunteers, college students, and members of [RCP] . . ."[88]

He goes on to say that the RCP assumed control of this effort but ran into dissension at the leadership level and reverted to destructive tactics which denied the Tenants' Union any success in its initial objectives, giving the RCP a forum for spreading its inflammatory doctrine.

Members of the collectives in San Jose were expected to support themselves and the RCP. With the exception of one individual whose RCP duties were considered too time-consuming for him to hold an outside job, everyone was expected to earn money while carrying out the work of infiltrating industry. Those not having families to support were expected to turn over to RCP 25% of their wages. Those with families were expected to contribute 7%. No one was supposed to have more than $200 in a personal bank account—anything over this amount was to be turned in to RCP. Members of the collectives maintained their own living quarters, but all were considered to be the property of RCP and available for meetings and for storing RCP materials. The residences were checked periodically to see that there was no evidence of luxury or extravagant spending. These inspections were supplemented by monthly financial statements members were required to submit to the treasurer of each collective.

All members were urged to obtain all possible government benefits for which they could qualify—food stamps, educational grants, etc. Those whose parents possessed substantial financial resources were urged to obtain gifts or subsidy allowances from home to be used for RCP purposes. When members of the RCP were arrested, other members with influential parents or those with well-established jobs were expected to assist in raising bail money and meeting legal expenses. Another source of income for RCP in the San Jose area was from the sale of the newspaper, *Salt of the Earth,* (originally named *Maverick.*) Each RCP member was expected to pay for a personal copy and to sell a quota each month to students, workers and people in the community not affiliated with RCP. Other sources of income included the proceeds from the sale of literature produced in China and "wholesaled" to RCP at a token cost, "commissions" on tour fees for Peking-arranged trips to China, and funds produced by front organizations.

The FBI informers stated that the biggest expenditures made by RCP were for weapons, ammunition and explosives. All members were required to have weapons in their homes and to be proficient with handguns, shotguns and semi-automatic carbines. Members were required to be willing to kill, and to fight to overthrow the existing U.S. system. In its literature, the RCP describes itself as:

". . . a national communist organization made up mainly of workers and students, Black, Brown, Asian, Native American and white. Our immediate program is to bring together, under the leadership of the working class, the main spearheads of struggle against the U.S. imperialist system . . . The long-range goal of this United Front

Against Imperialism, led by the working class, is to overthrow the dictatorship of the handful of monopoly capitalists (imperialists) and to establish the dictatorship of the working class, the great majority society, to build toward socialism and communism . . . To do this, we must join together into a single Communist Party, with the discipline, division of labor, and strategy and tactics capable of leading the immediate struggle of the people to deal the death blow to the imperialist system."[89]

In 1972, the Congressional report on RCP identified branches in some 25 localities of 9 states, and estimated the total membership to be about 400. The states in which branches were identified were: California, Illinois, Michigan, New Hampshire, New Jersey, New York, Ohio, Oregon and Pennsylvania. From the organization's literature, as well as from descriptions by informers, it seems that RCP does "secret work" in addition to its "legal work." The implication is that there are secret and illegal activities. The Hoover Institution estimates that RCP's 1978 membership was 2,000. The research for the present study indicated at least 40 locations—in Alabama, Colorado, Georgia, Massachusetts, Maryland, Texas, Washington, Wisconsin and Washington, D.C.—in addition to the states listed above. *Alternative America* showed only 9 locations, and the *Movement Mailing List*, three times that many. Others were found in RCP literature and assumed from mention in the regular press of incidents where RCP forces were reported to be involved in busing disputes, wildcat strikes, disruption of union activities, fighting in the streets with Iranian dissidents, and participating in such protests as those at Kent State University. The RCP lost some of its membership when it fell out of favor with Peking, but it seems that most of the defectors simply transferred to the rival Maoist organization, CP(ML), which is not unlike RCP in its organization, tactics and goals.[90]

FOUR

Alternative Issues

Miscellaneous Support Services for Alternative Media

One of the directories used in this study is published by the Alternative Press Syndicate (formerly the Underground Press Syndicate). It has never produced news for its member publications as does a conventional "wire service," but it has served to promote the underground/alternative media. It is apparently a little too far-out culturally for some of today's more fastidious alternatives. It tends to reflect a preoccupation with marijuana and the outrageousness of the old undergrounds, and is said to have been instrumental in founding *High Times,* a magazine which serves as the authoritative guide to drugs and drug paraphernalia. It advertises *High Times* in its magazine, *Alternative Media:* "It's where dope, sex and politics melt, mingle and fuse into ideas too hot for the official culture to handle." And it also carries ads for political papers such as *In These Times.* The greatest coup on the part of the Underground/Alternative Press Syndicate was in arranging for the microfilming of its member papers for sale to public, university and college libraries. This was done in cooperation with Bell & Howell Corporation under an agreement that, according to APS, nets 35% of the microfilm sales price for the Alternative Press Syndicate and its member papers. Through this arrangement, the underground/alternative ideas and materials are given a wider audience and the papers receive financial support.

Internationalism, mailed out of New York, is a quarterly for theory on "International Communist Current." It is listed in *Alternative America* as merely "political" but seems to be regarded by *Guardian* as a source of current thinking about the international communist scene.

Liberation News Service was founded in 1967 with the idea of providing "Movement News to Underground Papers." Two young college graduates, one from Amherst and one from Boston University, started it in Washington after they had been rejected in their bid to head the U.S. Student Press Association, having been "considered too freaky, too irresponsible." Laurence Leamer writes that "They were a curious duo—dope-smoking, hip, full of far-out incredulousness, yet terribly concerned about Vietnam, the urban crisis and politics." They were not Marxists, however. The indications are that they had no ideology of any sort. Perhaps "freaky and irresponsible" was an apt description. They soon were subject to sharp criticism from what they termed "vulgar Marxists," and LNS was split, existing for a short time as two versions of the same idea. The Marxists eventually won out and LNS became a collective of about a dozen young people working in New York "in the basement of a soot-stained apartment house, behind barred doors, shaded windows and a double-locked door."[91] By their own statements they were interested in sending out packets of "propaganda" against "imperialism" and in support of "liberation" at home and abroad. LNS has had a precarious financial base so that the "news packets" might be sent out as often as three times a week or, at times, only once a week. The main source of income has been charges to subscribers, most recently $240 a year for alternative media, $360 for libraries, and $500 for commercial users. In 1977 the list had shrunk to 169 domestic and 81 foreign subscribers, the latter dispersed among 25 countries, including Australia, Canada, England and France, as well as Cuba, the People's Republic of China and Soviet Russia. The American subscribers include a number of the publications discussed above: *Dollars & Sense; Seven Days; Guardian; Monthly Review;* the North American Congress on Latin America; *Win* magazine; the Middle East Research Information Project; the IPS offshoot, *Southern Exposure; In These Times;* the *Free Venice Beachhead;* the *Black Panther; Weekly People;* and *Peoples World.* The LNS subscription list also includes a number of radio stations generally counted among the alternative media: WMSC-FM in New Jersey; New York City's WBAI; WZBI-FM at Gettysburg College and WUHY of Philadelphia, in Pennsylvania; WPFW-PACIFICA in Washington, D.C.; WVSP-FM in North Carolina; WRFN in Nashville, Tennessee; WYSO at Antioch College in Ohio; and KTOO in Alaska, are examples.[92]

Tricontinental News Service, operating out of New York City, is another subscriber service which deals in "anti-imperialist" material. In this case, it excerpts and reprints commentary by the forces "struggling for liberation" in Asia, Africa and Latin America—hence, "tricontinental." The material includes "news and features" from alternative media in those areas of the world as well as reports from representatives of U.S. alternatives living or traveling in those areas.

Resist, headquartered in Cambridge, Massachusetts publishes a newsletter but its primary function with respect to the alternative media has been providing funds. It was formed in 1967 to provide financial aid to organizations and publications promoting draft resistance, but has since extended its interests to seeking donations for "social change" of various kinds, and redistributing these funds to leftist projects all over the country. Among the recipients of its grants are the Liberation News Service, *Liberation* magazine, *Radical America,* and the publishing activities of the Communist Party (Marxist-Leninist).

Alternatives for the Professions

There are alternative publications that serve various fields of science. The following descriptions indicate some of the more prominent ones.

The Bulletin of the Atomic Scientists was founded in the 1950s by American scientists whom Bouscaren and Lyon credit with "good intentions, trust and open-mindedness" about the sharing of scientific information internationally, aware of the "nature of the Communist conspiracy" but later discovering that to share with Soviet "scientists" meant to share with the Soviet government. Ralph de Toledano wrote that after initially believing Russian scientists approached their professions in the same way as Western scientists, the founding editor of the *Bulletin* discovered that the Soviet Academy of Science is simply a part of the Soviet government. Petr Beckmann observed that many of the scientists in the *Bulletin's* constituency "have long since forsaken science for politics, and the latter blatantly antinuclear." Examination of issues of the publication suggests that Beckmann is correct. The pages are often used to promote the radical-controlled antinuclear-power movement, and scientific matters seem to be of secondary importance.[93]

The *Bulletin of Concerned Asian Scholars* was founded in May, 1968 to support "anti-imperialist scholarship." Catalogues of Vocations for Social Change described it in the early 1970s as the publication of "a national political organization of students and faculty interested in Asia and in changing the concepts and purposes of current scholarship on Asia." Muller and Spahn's *From Radical Left to Extreme Right* describes it as challenging work that has previously been done on Asia in the social sciences and other disciplines. The *Bulletin* has cooperated with *Mother Jones* on some of that magazine's anticapitalist efforts, and was listed as a resource in the anticapitalist *Corporate Action Guide.* Its parent organization, the Committee of Concerned Asian Scholars, has aligned itself with various radical and far-left campaigns. Although it includes some nonradical scholars, it is generally "anti-Establishment" and substantially to the left of center.

The *Review of Radical Political Economics* and a subsidiary publication called *Dollars & Sense* are products of the Union for Radical Political Economics, founded by SDS leaders. The *Review* uses the rhetoric of Marxism, whereas *Dollars & Sense* is written in a lighter vein, designed to attract audiences in the broad population, and to promote the antibusiness themes of the Institute for Policy Studies.

Science for the People is the bimonthly magazine of Scientists and Engineers for Social and Political Change. VSC's *Resources Catalogue* describes the magazine as offering a "progressive-radical view on science and technology" and as being devoted "to challenging and proposing alternatives to the use of science as a tool for political and economic exploitation." It is plainly anticapitalistic, appears as a resource in the *Corporate Action Guide,* and is involved in the antinuclear-power movement.

State and Mind is described by *Resources Catalogue* as a "journal of radical therapy . . . that exposes the abuses and oppression perpetrated by the mental health industry . . . emphasizes alternatives to psychiatric establishment, such as self-help." It is said to be devoted to "integrating humanistic psychology and political consciousness." This is the third name this publication has had since it first appeared in 1971 as the *Radical Therapist.* Its first mailing address was a post office box in Minot, South Dakota, listing on its masthead the Radical Therapist, Inc. as its publisher. This was subsequently changed, along with the name of the publication to *Rough Times* and moved to a post office box address in West Somerville, Massachusetts where it is still published. The early issues of the publication show it to have been thoroughly involved in the underground press, and in "women's liberation" and "gay rights." Basically, it has supported radical social workers and psychologists who combine left politics with mental health programs and "rap centers."

Religious Alternatives

The *New York Times* of Sunday, July 16, 1978, devoted some twenty column inches to a story headline: "Evangelical Christian Movement Being Reshaped by Radical Wing." It read in part:

> "The evangelical Christian movement, the most powerful religious force in the nation, is being reshaped, largely as a result of the growing impact of values and themes once associated with the youth counterculture of the 1960s . . .
>
> Among the organized efforts to link evangelical faith with social

action are a broad-based group called Evangelicals for Social Action, several religious communities—among them, the 'Other Side' in Philadelphia—that espouse a total religious lifestyle and many youth groups such as 'Young Life' that have steadily turned toward activism.

Another measure of the interest in activism is the circulation boom among magazines that articulate the cause. The most widely known periodical, *Sojourners,* increased its circulation from 5,000 to 35,000 in two years, and the *Other Side* magazine has doubled its subscriptions in the last year . . . ."

Both of these publications turned up in our survey. *Sojourners,* which has on its masthead and among its by-lines some impressive names in evangelical circles, is listed in *Alternative America* and in the highly militant *Resources Catalogue.* And although it is published in Washington, D. C. and the *Other Side* is published in Philadelphia, the two magazines have some staff members in common.

The *New York Times* is correct about the boom in the circulation of radical religious magazines. They are multiplying as well as growing. *Signs of the Times,* describing itself as "A Journal for Socialist Christians" was founded in 1978. *Christianity and Crisis* is not new and does not appear in the directories, but its circulation is reported now as above 20,000. These are all nondenominational or, as they often call themselves, "ecumenical" publications. There are some overtly radical denominational publications, not listed in the directories, but unquestionably far left and "anti-Establishment." The Episcopal-related magazine, the *Witness,* and the Methodist *SQB (Social Questions Bulletin)* are examples.

With the exception of *SQB,* all of these publications seem to look for guidance or materials from the Institute for Policy Studies. This is especially true of *Sojourners* and the *Witness.* The *Witness* has drawn heavily on IPS, and *Sojourners* seems to be very close to Richard Barnet, one of the two co-founders of IPS. *SQB,* on the other hand, has shown a particular affinity for the US-China Peoples Friendship Association, some of its personnel helping to arrange meetings for the Association.

In general, these publications are antibusiness, if not blatantly anticapitalist; oriented toward "liberation theology" (that is, supportive of revolutionary efforts in Asia, Africa and Latin America); pro-women's liberation; proabortion; antiwar; even antidefense, and especially antinuclear, both in weapons and power production; opposed to intelligence-gathering activities; and more or less prohomosexual. On this last issue, they seem to have a problem, and they are cautious. If they take a firm stand against homosexuality, they will lose their standing in radical circles. On the other hand, if they do not admit some Biblical injunctions against it, they will lose their credibility among deeply religious people — and that is the audience most of them seek to influence. *Christianity and Crisis* dealt with the issue in this manner:

> "Moving closer to the core of the issue, we submit further that something is badly out of kilter when the physical character of sexual practices, considered wholly apart from the emotions and commitment these practices may express, is accepted as sufficient grounds for moral condemnation. The real theological problem, we believe, is not that of reconciling acceptance of homosexuality with the scriptural passages that appear to condemn it, but rather how to reconcile condemnation of homosexuals with the criteria of morality that are truly central to the Christian message. In determining human and ethical uses of sex, it is not the laws of biology we must consult but the law of love. To say this is not to relativize the scriptures or to make our burdens light; on the contrary, it is a hard saying . . . It is our view, however, that in the church the burden of proof rests on those who would maintain the policy of condemnation and ostracism that is our inheritance. And we believe that not the last consequence of a shift in the policy will be liberation and enlightenment for ourselves."[94]

The magazine, the *Other Side,* openly waffles on the issue. The lead editorial, in an edition it devoted entirely to the homosexual issue, read:

> "The *Other Side* has spent more than nine months working on this special issue. We hoped as a staff to come to a full agreement among ourselves on the questions of homosexual behavior and heterosexual response. Many times we were close to that agreement — but always the agreement fell apart.

> We all firmly adhere to the authority of Scripture. And, as a result, we all firmly believe that most homosexual behavior is contrary to God's standards. Our differences concern the legitimacy — or illegitimacy — of permanent, faithful homosexual relationships for people who feel they have no other viable sexual alternative . . . Because of our internal disagreements, no article or column should be construed as an official position of the *Other Side.* The opinions expressed are those of the authors."[95]

This same publication has no such compunctions in its "anti-Establishment " stance, although as with the majority of the alternative publications in this study, it is vague about its actual political and economic objectives. It reaches for credibility by denouncing the Soviet Union and "state socialism," but does not hesitate to attack capitalism in favor of some vaguely articulated utopian socialist concept. The following is typical:

> "We radical Christians are best known for our fierce commitment to social justice. We believe that the social situation in America is so gross that basic (radical) change is absolutely essential. It is true that internally many countries (Chile, Uganda, South Africa, Kampuchea and the Soviet Union) are at least as unjust as the U. S., but that is no reason for complacency. Racism, poverty, sexism, classism, and environmental destruction are pervasive in the U. S. and only fundamental structural change can correct that. And the changes we are calling for go off the scale of America's two-party system."

Elsewhere in this edition the reader is offered a scale for rating himself as a "radical Christian." He gets 100 points for agreeing that "America stinks" and is penalized 100 points if he insists "America is the greatest," 200 points are scored if "you live in a community" and 300 are deducted if "you live in the suburbs." 300 points are awarded for narrow-mindedness and a penalty of 300 points for broad-mindedness. The ideological confusion is further manifest in the continuation of the passage cited above:

> "What is more, if you look at America's foreign relations, things are even more appalling. Never in history has such a military monster existed. (Not that we are peculiarly wicked, only that we are peculiarly powerful.) Our nuclear arsenal (whether 'peaceful' or as weapons) seems almost certain (eventually) to contribute to blowing up the world. And our military forces (undercover and in uniform) combined with our economic might have installed or propped up gulag archipelagos throughout the third world. All this, as we see it, has been done not in the interests of the American people. It has been done because it is in the interests of a handful of interlocking corporations. We distribute thumb screws in the third world so American companies can get richer selling us oil and sugar that destroy our environment and damage our bodies. Such is the price of prosperity.
>
> This analysis has forced radicals to conclude that one of our prime tasks is to work toward dismantling the economic power that resides in the hands of a few. Most of us have not moved toward state socialism. (It also leaves too much power in the hands of too few.) Rather we tend toward trustbusting and cooperatives. Most of us believe that small is beautiful; economic structures must be shaped as if people mattered."[96]

The articles in *Sojourners* are generally well-written statements of liberal intellectualism utilizing Biblical references and quotations. As noted earlier, this publication presents some well-known authors and public figures. For example, Senator Mark Hatfield has a by-line in the January 1977 edition—and he is listed on the magazine's masthead as a contributing editor. His article is basically a plea for return to personal responsibility and accountability, in one place referring to Dr. Karl Menninger's book, *Whatever Became of Sin?*, and he concludes with the following passage after having expressed his concern about the greed for power:

> "There are other sins that abound in our modern society which we should examine—lying, stealing, cheating, taking what is not one's own and all the contemporary forms of narcotic self-indulgence. These are sins that go on at all levels of society, in our corporations, in our finest schools, in our churches and everywhere else.
>
> Included are all of the compromises with integrity which are so easily rationalized in our contemporary life in the name of getting ahead . . .
>
> In every case, what is called for is a change of heart—for people to turn around, to be converted, to receive the good news, to be forgiven, to be accepted, to encounter Christ. And in each case we are called to a renewal of society, to corporate repentance, to justice, to relief of the suffering, 'to proclaim release of the captives, to set at liberty those who are oppressed,' as the scripture states. That must be the shape of the evangelistic mission in our time and our land."[97]

But the editor of *Sojourners,* Jim Wallis, sees things rather differently:

> "There has been much confusion about the meaning of conversion, especially where contemporary evangelicalism has been most widely discussed. People are being called to Christ in an historical vacuum. We have forgotten that a relationship to Christ means a relationship to the purposes of Christ in history . . .
>
> The evangelical tradition has the capacity to fundamentally challenge the American status quo and to offer a fresh corporate vision of justice and peace firmly rooted in the biblical witness. But, thus far, the present evangelical revival has shown a characteristically evangelical preference for proclaiming personal virtue while ignoring its conformity to the most basic economic and political realities of the American power structure.
>
> Evangelicals still seem to believe that the spread of personal piety is still the most reliable standard for a nation's morality. What the evangelical movement has yet failed to say is that the biblical demands for justice and compassion bring the harshest kind of judgment to the system of wealth and power upon which the society is based . . .

A revival of genuine biblical faith in this country may in fact provide the strongest foundation and resources for social criticism and social change. For while the Judaeo-Christian heritage has consistently been distorted to serve the interests of those in power, it is that same heritage that offers the most fundamental kind of challenge to the prevailing order.

A whole new generation of radical Christians may turn America's traditional affirmation of the biblical tradition on its head. That biblical heritage can then be used to attack the system rather than defend it. It is these biblical seeds of protest, political resistance, social change, and alternative vision that could most threaten the present American status quo. An American radicalism that is biblically based and conceived in the churches could be a far more serious threat to the established order in America than political responses that are based on secular ideology."[98]

It is not surprising, therefore, that *Sojourners* castigates a number of the more visible evangelists—Charles Colson, Bill Bright, and above all, Anita Bryant. Its heroes are Kim Chi Ha, the Catholic dissident in South Korea who is credited with this remarkable statement: "I believe in nonviolence, but I also approve the violence of love and regulated violence";[99] David Truong, the Vietnamese recently convicted of passing classified documents stolen by a U.S. government employee to officials in the "New Vietnam"; Orlando Letelier, the Chilean diplomat at the time of Allende and until his death, associated with the Institute for Policy Studies; and various priests and bishops in Latin America who espouse Marxism and revolution. The priorities of *Sojourners* may be further surmised from a ten-day retreat in which its editor and senior staff members discussed "Survival and the Gospel" with the radical leftist Sidney Lens. Lens has extensive credentials in radical politics and organizing, is a leader in the communist-dominated segment of the antiwar movement, and an instigator of the present antinuclear movement. If he has any credentials as a religious authority, they have been rather well-concealed.

In this connection, it is interesting to note that *Sojourners* is published by the Peoples Christian Coalition, located in the building which housed antiwar headquarters—including those of the Peoples Coalition for Peace and Justice associated with the Peoples Party, of which Sidney Lens was the Chicago area head. Such associations are never definitive, but it is significant that *Sojourners* is given space in the *Resources Catalogue* which carries only the purest far-left organizations and publications.

One other religious alternative is worthy of special note. It is *Radical Religion*, which describes its origin and mission:

"*Radical Religion* grew out of the Berkeley Free Church. With the dissolution of the Church, *Radical Religion* was established as an autonomous publication of the Radical Religion Collective, now called the Community for Religious Research and Education.

The quarterly's goal is to serve as a radical alternative to existing theoretical journals, exploring such areas as the role of religion in the larger movement for revolutionary change, the rediscovery of humanity's rich radical religious heritage, the commitment of radicals to socialism, the relationship between politically active social Christianity, and the ways in which traditional religions embody world views compatible with radical new forms of liberation. The primary focus of *Radical Religion* is within Judaeo-Christian tradition, but we are actively seeking and welcome contributions from individuals and groups within other traditions."[100]

This magazine is something on the order of a wholesale outlet for radical religious theory. It is written for people who are already involved in "radical religion," not in the subtle tones of the publications designed to draw recruits into the movement. It offers quotations of Mao Tsetung and Che Guevara on its pages occasionally, and assumes the reader is acquainted with the basic ideas of Marxism and "socialism," which it seeks to place in a religious framework. A topical theme is chosen for each issue of the magazine. Recently the subject was "Reconsidering Popular Religion." Major articles included: "Feminism, Liberation Theology and Socialism"; "Class Origins and Class Readings of the Bible"; and "Feminism and Socialism," with particular stress on the ordination of women for the ministry.

The Berkeley Free Church, out of which *Radical Religion* grew, described itself as an "ecumenical ministry to transient youth, street people" providing "drug and legal referral, housing, free food, information" and "occasional worship." It claimed to "work closely with the First Baptist Church," to be concerned with "peace and ecology action" and to have ties with "tenants' unions and the Black Panthers." An adjunct to this operation was Free Church Publications which probably was the incubator for *Radical Religion.* Among the works published by FCP are: *The Liberated Zone: A Guide to Christian Resistance,* by John Pairman Brown; *The Covenant of Peace: A Liberation Prayer Book,* compiled by John Pairman Brown and Richard L. York; and *Win with Love: A Comprehensive Directory of the Liberated Church,* published with the assistance of Vocations for Social Change—the Marxist collective that produced the *Resources Catalogue* directory.

Brown's book *The Liberated Zone* comprises five separately written papers, one of which he describes as a report to "the Episcopal Peace Fellowship who helped me go around the world via Prague and Hanoi in the fall of 1967—as well as to my patient SDS traveling companions." His conclusion in Chapter V, "Church Renewal and the Peace Movement," is that the church will be renewed when capitalist exploitation is ended and the "convergence of Christianity and Marxism twists together two strands temporarily frayed from the same thread."

The Covenant of Peace is a 200-page parody of the Episcopal Prayer Book focusing on the events and heroes and heroines of the civil rights and antiwar movements, the Russian, Chinese and Cuban revolutions, and the romanticism of guerrilla warfare.

Win with Love is 125 pages of a directory of 835 locations of radical organizations in the 50 U. S. states, the District of Columbia and Puerto Rico, and 17 foreign countries. Although the subtitle is "A Comprehensive Directory of the Liberated Church" and it does list scattered local churches and elements of the national headquarters of most of the better-known denominations and religious bodies in the country, about half of its entries are organizations that could scarcely be considered religious—Black Panthers, Friends of the Earth, Liberation News Service, National Welfare Rights Organization, United Farm Workers, Vocations for Social Change and the War Resisters League. It does offer something of a profile of the denominations which have had substantial involvement with radical organizations. Compiled in 1970-71, it provides historical perspective about some of the radical religious activities of today, as indicated by the following sampling of the listings:

102. The Community of Christ, Washington, D.C.
     John Schramm, pastor; Rosemary Reuther.
     Ecumenical community, once mostly Lutheran and Catholic, meeting Fri. and Sat. They dissolve and renew their covenant twice a year. Coffeehouse and bookstore open weekdays. Tutoring program, interclass Montessori school.

240. Methodist Federation for Social Action, Ardsley, N.Y.
     Rev. Lee H. Ball, exec. secy.
     Independent Methodist group since 1907. Historic concern for civil liberties, socialism; interchange with Hiroshima, India, E. Germany, USSR. Monthly *SQB-Social Questions Bulletin.*

244. World Fellowship, Inc., Bronx, N.Y.
     W. Christopher Schmauch, exec. dir.
     Group working for world government and peace. They sponsor dialogues with Marxist humanism; Gandhi observances; study tours to E. Berlin; USSR, W. Africa. Conference center at Kerhonkson, N.Y.

269. Episcopal Peace Fellowship, New York, N.Y.
     Susan Miller and David Vance, co-directors.
     National education and action group coordinating local chapters, some here listed. They sponsored the Pentagon Masses in 1970. Lobbying inside Episcopal structure, especially for

abolition of military chaplaincy.

274. Merton-Buber House, New York, N.Y.
Paul Grazier, contact person.
Coalition from Christianity, Judaism, humanism who believe in brotherhood of man; concerned with racism, poverty. Military, draft counseling, nonviolence.

347. Philadelphians for Equal Justice, Philadelphia, Pa.
Rev. David Gracie, contact person.

460. Another Mother for Peace, Beverly Hills, Ca.
Dorothy B. Jones, contact person.
Postal network of 175,000 women with newsletter. They broke the story of offshore oil leases in S.E. Asia. Posters, etc.: "War is not healthy for children and other living things."

482. Justice/Action/Peace in Latin America (JAPLA)
Glenn E. Smiley, exec. secy.
Working for nonviolent revolution in Latin America throughout publications, teach-ins, direct action. Supported by National Council of Churches.

501. Council on Religion and the Homosexual, San Francisco, Ca.
Phyllis Lyon, vice president.
Education agency via media, symposia. Special concern for police-community relations.

538. Church of the Saviour, Washington, D.C.
N. Gordon Cosby and every member, ministers.
Ecumenical congregation stressing annual recommitment; School of Christian Living; many outreach enterprises here and overseas; associated from Dayspring. Pioneer in free-church movement.

550. Peoples Coalition for Peace and Justice, Washington, D.C.
Continues New Mobe & National Coalition Against War, Racism & Repression. Now cooperating with Southern Christian Leadership Conference and National Welfare Rights Organization.

598. Seminarians for Ministerial Renewal, Chicago, Ill.
Vince Champagne, national coordinator.
Catholic based, but ecumenical. Extensive international network gathering information and building for action. Alternate models for education; struggle for optional celibacy.

725. American Committee on Africa, New York, N.Y.
Research, defense and aid fund, liberation support, lobbying against Gulf Oil support of Angola.

805. National Lawyers Guild, Philadelphia Office.
Dick Lavine and Harry Levitan, contact people.
Local office for communication with the movement for radical
social change. Among other cases they are doing antipolice
suits. Newsletter, pamphlets.

807. Philadelphia Task Force on Women in Religion.
Public panels and other action. Newsletter *Genesis Three* with
news and book reviews. Both Christian and Jewish members.

The numbers are the catalogue numbers in the directory. No. 102
mentions Rosemary Reuther who is now a speaker and writer in radical
religious circles and serves as a contributing editor to *Christianity and
Crisis.* In her endorsement of the *Witness,* she is described as "the
feminist theologian at Garrett Theological Seminary." To update No.
240, one would have to add to the list of interchanges the People's
Republic of China, because key members of this group have been
involved in tours to Peking sponsored by the US-China Peoples
Friendship Association. The Dorothy B. Jones listed in No. 460 signed
the "Call to Action" that precipitated the antinuclear umbrella
organization, the Mobilization for Survival. Numbers 482 and 501 deal
with completely different issues but are both illustrative of matters
which were commonly advocated in the underground/alternative media
long before they were ever mentioned in the regular press. Rev. Gordon
Cosby, listed in No. 538, has had his by-line in *Sojourners,* and the
magazine also lists his church as that attended by the Institute for
Policy Studies co-founder and writer in many radical religious
publications, Richard Barnet. Number 725 also illustrates the concerns
and activities that became prominent in the underground/alternative
media before they were mentioned elsewhere.

It is clear that the early agitation and organizing of groups on this
list led to the subsequent widespread attack on corporations in the
name of religious causes. An examination of two of the handbooks
developed by radicals to promote such attacks, *Corporate Action Guide,*
and *Struggling with the Energy System — Probing Alternatives,* reveals
an extensive list of church-related organizations recommended as "resources." The first of these two handbooks on anticapitalist tactics was
published by the Corporate Action Project in Washington in 1974, the
other was published by the staff of the radical Episcopalian publication,
the *Witness,* with help from the Institute for Policy Studies.

Listings in these two "resources" include:

American Christians Toward Socialism (ACTS)
1800 Hartwell, Detroit, MI 48235

(National organization with local chapters whose members have strong roots in the Christian tradition and share a growing commitment to socialism. Involved in study and local political action.)

American Friends Service Committee
160 North 15th Street, Philadelphia, Pa. 19102
(Pacifist service organization. Offices in major cities.)

B-1 Bomber, National Peace Conversion Campaign
Clergy and Laity Concerned
235 East 49th St.
New York, N.Y. 10017
American Friends Service Committee
[address as above]

Bread for the World
235 East 49th St., New York, N.Y. 10017
(A Christian movement which seeks to impact on the hunger problem through pressure on government leaders. Local study and action groups. National network.)

Church Research and Information Projects (CRIPS)
Box 223, Cathedral Station, New York, N.Y. 10025
(Gathers, analyzes and circulates information and educational materials on religion and society which relate to the liberation of the oppressed.)

Corporate Information Center
National Council of Churches
475 Riverside Drive, New York, N.Y. 10027
(Publishes strongly antibusiness monthly magazine the *Corporate Examiner.*)

IMPACT
110 Maryland Ave., N.E. Washington, D.C. 20002
(Interfaith National Legislative Information Network. Issues background papers for legislative follow-up; suggests action for immediate political response.)

Interfaith Center on Corporate Responsibility
475 Riverside Drive, New York, N.Y. 10027
(Monitors social effects of corporations' policies. Works to influence corporate policy through dialogue and stockholder resolutions.)

Interfaith Committee on Social Responsibility in Investments
475 Riverside Drive, Rm. 566, New York, N.Y. 10027

Joint Strategy and Action Committee (JSAC)
475 Riverside Drive, New York, N.Y. 10027
(Publishes "anti-Establishment" monthly *JSAC Grapevine.*)

Methodist Federation for Social Action
Shalom House, 76 Clinton Ave., Staten Island, N.Y.
(This Methodist network is engaged in study and activities very
similar to those being undertaken by the Church and Society
Network.)

National Action Research on the Military-Industrial Complex
(NARMIC)
American Friends Service Committee
160 North 15th St., Philadelphia, Pa. 19102

National Catholic Coalition for Responsible Investments Justice
and Peace Center
3900 North 3rd Street, Milwaukee, Wis. 53212

Network
224 D St., S.E., Washington, D.C. 20003
(National membership of religious women working on social justice
issues through influence on national legislation. Lead workshops
for local groups on how to go about lobbying and impacting social
change.)

The mere listing in one of these handbooks does not automatically
qualify a group as "anti-Establishment" or far left, but the nature of
the handbooks is such that any organization which *knowingly* allies
itself with their goals can hardly be regarded as committed to traditional
American institutions. Finally, it should be noted that the phrase
"Church and Society" is one regularly used by radical groups of many
religious denominations and ecumenical organizations.

The Sex Role in Alternative Media

This study has focused at length on the alternative media dealing with
politics. Publications in this category constitute about 7% of the total.
Other topics, such as *schools, food* and *ecology* are listed in about the
same frequency. Among the next categories in frequency, at approximately 5% each, are *consumerism, communities, cooperatives* and
book publishing and selling. Of greater prominence, accounting for 8%
of the total, are organizations and publications concerned with sex
roles in the society—women, men, lesbians, homosexuals. This category
is dominated overwhelmingly by entries concerned with female rights
and roles. For example, in the most comprehensive of the directories,
Alternative America, there are just over 400 dealing with the female,
and less than 40 dealing with the male. Of the 157 publications (as

distinct from organizations) in this category, 143 were female-oriented. Among male-oriented publications, two-thirds have some emphasis on homosexuality. Of the 143 female-oriented, 56 are are least partially advocates of lesbianism.

Among the more influential publications in the survey are *Ms.*, about which comments have been made above; *Off Our Backs*, one of the older ones and formerly counted in the ranks of the underground papers; *Majority Report*, which is newer, larger but quite as militant and vulgar; and the *Women's Rights Law Reporter*. Others include: *Country Women*, published by a women's collective in Mendocino County, California, and written up in *Mother Jones* as having a circulation of 10,000; *Feminist Studies*, published within the Women's Studies Program at the University of Maryland; *Le'sbeinformed*, published by the Lesbian Resource Center, Inc. in Minneapolis; *Lesbian Tide*, published in Los Angeles; *Sisters*, from San Francisco; and the *Women's International Network News*, coming out of Lexington, Massachusetts. All of these publications qualify as being *feminist* but none would be judged very *feminine* in the traditional meaning of that term. Indeed, among these publications there is a scarcity of serious analyses of what *values* the "women's movement" does espouse.

In 1973, in his book *Sexual Suicide,* George Gilder described the women's movement as being destined to destroy much of the traditional value system, including the family, and to push some young men toward homosexuality. The book has, of course, been attacked by feminists but it is thought-provoking and, as yet, unanswered in its contentions. A more recent book, with something of the same focus, but concerning itself more with media content and government action in support of feminism is entitled *The Assault on the Sexes* by Jim and Andrea Fordham, a husband-wife writing team living in the suburbs of Washington, D.C. One of the points made by the Fordhams is that the impression which the general public has of the "women's rights" movement is dramatically different from the pronouncements of the militant advocates of feminism and "women's liberation." The Fordhams claim "most people just are not aware of the deep-down radical nature of this movement." This lack of awareness prevails, they add, despite the fact that in their own literature, activist feminists are very candid about their objectives. Throughout the range of subjects espoused by the alternative press, there is a significant gap between what the activists proclaim in their own circles and what the public perceives to be at issue. This disparity is of such importance that it is well to illustrate it with material provided by the Fordhams.

The first is a passage they quote from Kate Millett's book *Sexual Politics*. It is well to remember that it was published in 1970, before the idea of "women's lib" had extended much beyond the feminist circles in which Kate Millett wrote and spoke, when she probably had no thought that these ideas in more subtle language would permeate the "Establishment" media (and thus the society) to the extent they have:

"In America one may expect the new women's movement to ally itself on an equal basis with blacks and students in a growing radical coalition. It is also possible that women now represent a very crucial element capable of swinging the national mood, poised at this moment between the alternative of progress or political repression, toward meaningful change. As the largest alienated element in our society, and because of their number, passion and length of oppression, its largest revolutionary base, women might come to play a leadership part in social revolution, quite unknown before in history. The changes in fundamental values such as a coalition of expropriated groups— blacks, youth, women, the poor—would seek are especially pertinent to realizing not only sexual revolution but a gathering impetus toward freedom from rank or prescriptive role, sexual or otherwise."[101]

Another citation in *The Assault on the Sexes* is from *Sisterhood Is Powerful: An Anthology of Writings from the Women's Liberation Movement.* Under a section headed "How Will the Family Be Destroyed?" Revolutionary Communist Party member Roxanne Dunbar is quoted as writing:

"After all, women must take care of the children, and there will continue to be children. Our demand for full-time child care in the public schools will be met to some degree all over, and perhaps fully in places. The alleviation of the duty of full-time child care in private situations will free many women to make decisions they could not before. But more than that, the demand alone will throw the whole ideology of the family into question, so that women can begin establishing a community of work with each other and we can fight collectively. Women will feel freer to leave their husbands and become economically independent, either through a job or welfare . . ."[102]

Then, actress Shirley MacLaine, who was on the first all women's US-China Peoples Friendship Association tour to Peking, is quoted as saying we should "help make socialism respectable, because that's where we've got to go now. We're seeing that capitalism hasn't worked," and "we should be banding together to socialize oil and steel and medicine and education . . . working to change values."[103] Also on changing values, Simone de Beauvoir, author of the nearly thirty-year-old book, *The Second Sex,* is quoted:

"No woman should be authorized to stay at home to raise her children. Women should not have that choice, precisely because if there is such a choice, too many women will make that one . . . Encouraging

91

women to stay at home will not change society . . . In my opinion, as long as the family and the myth of the family and the myth of maternity and maternal instinct are not destroyed, women will still be oppressed . . . We are trying to change society so that women who do happen to be the people who give birth, can be full people in society. A whole new approach to child-rearing needs to be created— not just mother, but mother, father, society as a whole, the communal situation, if you wish, and the child care center and so on . . ."[104]

One further quotation from alternative literature should be cited. It is an excerpt from a speech by RCP member Mary Lou Greenberg at the 1970 International Women's Day Celebration. As a member of RCP, she had something in common with Roxanne Dunbar and as a member of the US-China Peoples Friendship Association, she had something in common with Shirley MacLaine. She told her audience in San Francisco:

"Some people used to think that women's liberation meant a kind of personal liberation or freedom—the idea being that by going braless, living in a commune, sleeping around with many men instead of just one, a woman could be 'free.' The idea was that it was possible for individuals to be free before—or even without—changing the basic structure of our present society.

But more and more people are realizing that individual solutions are available only to the rich—that there's no such thing as individual freedom for the masses of people—male and female—in a slave society like the one we've got now. Only socialism, where the working people own the industries and run the government for the benefit of all of us, can offer liberation for women as well as for men . . .

. . . In Vietnam women had few rights before the Democratic Republic of Vietnam was established under Ho Chi Minh in 1946. After the French were defeated, women were given immediate voting rights. Today in North Vietnam women receive equal pay for equal work, and work in the fields and factories as well as fight alongside the men to defend their country . . .

To build that socialist society and the women's liberation which must be a part of it, we have to recognize who the enemy is. Our enemy is not men. Our enemy is U.S. imperialism—the bosses, the big corporation owners, the politicians who work for them, and the police and the army who protect their interests . . ."[105]

This is strong language. It is, however, describing the alternatives to present *fundamental values* as an extremist group visualizes them. Less militant alternative publications stop short of such extremist descriptions, but they do not give any real assurance that the extremist goal is not their ultimate purpose. Indeed, the alternative media and alternative organizations are full of talk about *change,* but generally they do not answer the question "Change to what?"

The Fordhams wrote in *The Assault on the Sexes:*

> "The trick of revolutionary fermentation is that it creates an unstable environment in which unexpected political shifts can happen before people know what is going on."[106]

History has repeatedly demonstrated that the breakdown of institutions is the precondition for the destruction of a political or social system. This phenomenon is generally perceived in terms of political or economic breakdown in which militants of either the left or right have seized power. The Fordhams have emphasized that *moral* chaos can also be the precursor of revolution. When there is a widespread confusion among the citizens about what is right and what is wrong, the resistance to militant advocacy of one cause or another diminishes. The assertion by Simone de Beauvoir that no woman should be "authorized to stay at home to raise her children" may have seemed absurd three decades ago. It is rapidly becoming a part of conventional wisdom in the United States today, most dramatically evident in the affirmative action policies of the government.

With insistent regularity, the alternative media have succeeded in converting aggressively promoted alternative values into legalisms. Repeatedly that which has been advanced as an alternative concept, or mode of behavior, has been eventually converted to a right which must then be protected by law. The placement of women in occupations once largely confined to men is a *right,* homosexuality is a *right,* welfare subsidy is a *right,* disrupting the construction of a power plant is a *right,* and so on.

Some Concluding Observations

The role of the alternative media has been to legitimize conduct and philosophies previously regarded as undesirable or inappropriate within the American ethos, and it has been phenomenally successful in this effort. The extent to which this legitimization is judged to have been desirable will depend upon the value priorities of the person making the judgment, but it will be a rare individual whose values have not been significantly altered during the last two decades. In other words, the changed basis for the citizen's judgments is a part of the change that has been wrought by the alternative press.

One thing is indisputable: the changes that have come about under pressure from the alternative media have led to the weakening of all the traditional institutions in which people are associated as private citizens—businesses, professions, families, churches, voluntary social service agencies, schools and clubs. In this process, the standards set by such institutions in order to fulfill their respective functions have been weakened, or in some cases outlawed, and the central government has increasingly been superimposed as the governing authority.

As the governance of an institution is transferred from the people directly involved in its activities to remote legislators and compliance officers, there is a double loss. The institution suffers from its incapacity to make direct judgments about, and respond to, local circumstances, and the obligations of the central government keep multiplying in the face of stark evidence that the government can no longer effectively fulfill or even pay for the obligations it has already assumed.

This change takes on added gravity when one recognizes that most of the alternative movement, which has been so influential in bringing about the new order, has no clear concept about how the machinery of the new society should be operated. (The segment of the alternative press that is formally allied with a specific political ideology is numerically not large.)

For the most part, the objectives achieved by the alternative movement have produced increasingly permissive behavior, disposing of the restraints that operate in one's private life, and in public life freeing the individual to use uncivil, coercive and/or destructive techniques in his efforts to bring about change. Apart from the impact which the new freewheeling conduct has had upon the institutions of society, there is the other large question of whether the increasing level of permissiveness has had a wholesome or destructive effect on the life experience of the individual citizen. Thoughtful observers have questioned whether the human psyche can withstand an existence in which there is no acknowledged difference between right and wrong, good and bad.

For the business community, this summary of the intentions and the power of the alternative movement may suggest that economic education is not a very effective mechanism for responding to the increasingly unfavorable national and international circumstances in which business must be conducted. The large problems are essentially cultural ones which cannot be resolved by responding to their political and economic manifestations. Michael Novak's *The American Vision*[107] offers a persuasive set of recommendations about what business leaders might do to hold their own in the increasingly hostile culture.

Finally, if actions should be undertaken to try to counteract the changes which the alternative movement has been so successful in promoting, such efforts will be hobbled and impeded by one aspect of the radical activity not touched upon thus far. Those who have advocated the alternatives have invariably done so under the banners of the loftiest and most fervent idealism. Each new venture has been insistently labeled "progress" or "freedom" or "justice" or "equality." The entire spectrum of morality has been hijacked and turned inside out. And too often, the efforts of the traditional institutions of society to block each new "alternative" campaign have been justified with arguments of *practical,* not *idealistic,* considerations.

The few leaders of countermovements who have insisted that the causes they were resisting were *wrong*—notably Phyllis Schlafly and Anita Bryant—have been attacked with a ferocity wholly unsuited to the discussion of issues in an open society. Having pre-empted all virtue, the alternative movement simply *cannot tolerate opposition based on a claim of idealism* and must marshal all forces to obliterate anyone so rash as to insist that an "alternative" cause is unjust or unethical.

For the most part, the leadership of the traditional institutions has grown unaccustomed to making judgments on the basis of right or wrong. Ideals, morals and ethics, like petticoats and spats, have fallen into disuse. However, the alternative movement, by its own performance, has revealed its Achilles' heel—it cannot tolerate claims and proof that idealism lies with the opposition, and anyone who would do battle with this immensely powerful and pervasive adversary would be well advised to develop his battle plan accordingly.

AFTERWORD

This analysis has been based on a direct examination of a number of the publications and a comparative analysis of five independently published directories, supplemented by specific references to other publications that have appeared in magazine and newspaper articles in both the "Establishment" and alternative media. Twenty-two percent of the publications on our list were examined directly. This was made possible by obtaining a number of the publications through the mail and examining others in libraries. Each of the five directories used was itself a product of the "alternative America" it catalogued:

> *Alternative America,* published by Resources, Cambridge, Mass., a computer-assisted compilation of 5,000 "lifestyle" and political organizations and publications nationwide.

> *Resources Catalogue: Media Connection,* published by Vocations for Social Change, Oakland, Ca., listing over 500 alternative "media projects" throughout the country.

> *Movement Mailing List,* compiled by Central Committee of Correspondence, Philadelphia, listing 2,000 "movement organizations and publications" throughout the country.

> *The Gazette Guide to National Organizations, National Alternative Media, D.C. Organizations & D.C. Media,* published by the *D.C. Gazette,* an alternative weekly in Washington, D.C., listing 1,200 organizations and publications considered to have national importance.

> *Alternative Media,* published by the Alternative Press Syndicate, New York City, listing its claimed 225 member publications.

Library research was conducted in the University of Wisconsin and Wisconsin State Historical libraries in Madison, the Library of

Congress, and in the public libraries in Virginia and Maryland adjacent to Washington, D.C. Supplementary checking with other libraries and media sources in other cities was made by telephone.

No single source was discovered that would reveal the entire underground/alternative media picture. Although highly useful, and finally more comprehensive than any other compilations, the directories cited above cannot be regarded as authoritative. Each of them listed publications as "current" that were out of print, and each failed to list some that were extant. Only comparison and direct examination or outside inquiry provide the researcher with confidence that his list approaches accuracy. The publications we are dealing with are too unorthodox and too nonconformist for any count to be other than approximate. The casualty rate has always been high among them, and few have ever been concerned with contributing to historical records.

The preparation of this text lasted more than a year so what was true at the time of writing may have been superseded by later events.

NOTES

Chapter One

The Origins of the Alternative Press

[1]Laurence Leamer, *The Paper Revolutionaries*, Simon & Schuster, New York, 1972, p. 83.

The 'Death' of the Alternative Press

[2]As was generally true of underground papers that folded, each of the papers here mentioned published a "swan song" edition, explaining why the paper was ceasing publication and giving some indication as to what the staff planned to do in the future. In most cases, finances or internal editorial problems were given as reasons, and members of the staff were said to be joining other projects in "the movement." In a few cases, there was something of an admission that the existing staff did not have the capability for publishing a more subtle, yet still politically effective paper, and was "going back to the books," perhaps to resume publication at some later date.

[3]*Orpheus*, August 1968, as cited by Robert J. Glessing, *The Underground Press in America*, Indiana University Press, Bloomington, Indiana, 1971, p. 4. (Incidentally, Tom Forcade committed suicide in New York City November 16, 1978.)

[4]*Scanlon's*, December 1969, p. 91. The interviewer was said to have been a radio news director in San Francisco who is named and quoted as describing himself as "well-known in the Bay Area for my leftist views." He is said to have received an anonymous phone call offering him the interview with the provisions that he allow himself to be picked up on a downtown street, blindfolded, and driven to a secret hideout. There he was allowed to question an unidentified young man who, in his judgment, was "middle class" and "college educated." He taped the interview, but his "hosts" transcribed it onto paper and burned the tape before he was again blindfolded and returned to the streets of San Francisco.

[5]Kirkpatrick Sale, *SDS*, Random House, N.Y., 1973, p. 558.

Undergrounds Become Alternatives

[6]*Northwest Passage*, Bellingham, Washington, July 9-July 30, p. 20.

[7]Summarized in a statement approved by the magazine's editor in *From Radical Left to Extreme Right*, by Robert H. Muller, et al., Campus Publishers, Ann Arbor, 1970.

[8]See additional information on the NCASLPP, starting on page 53.

Chapter Two

The Alternative Press Comes of Age

[9]*The New Yorker*, April 10, 1978, p. 118.

[10]*Los Angeles Times,* May 30, 1978, p. 1.

[11]*Washington Post,* July 2, 1978.

[12]The *Los Angeles Times* story reports "more than 50 alternative weeklies" now being published, but actually names less than half that number. *The New Yorker* names almost all of those and adds a few. Between the two publications, the following papers are reported as falling into the category of "alternative weeklies": *Alaska Advocate; Atlanta Gazette; Boston Phoenix; Chicago Reader; Creative Loafing,* Atlanta; *Figaro,* New Orleans; *Gris Gris,* Baton Rouge; *Hartford Advocate,* Connecticut; *Maine Times; Maui Sun,* Hawaii; *Monday,* Vancouver, B.C., Canada; *New Haven Advocate,* Connecticut; *New Times Weekly,* Phoenix, Arizona; *Pacific Sun,* Marin County, California; *The Real Paper,* Boston; *San Diego Reader; San Francisco Bay Guardian; Straight Creek Journal,* Denver; *Twin Cities Reader; Valley Advocate,* Amherst, Massachusetts; *The Weekly,* Seattle; and *Willamette Week,* Portland, Oregon.

[13]*Alternative Media,* Vol. 9, No. 6, Winter 1978, P.O. Box 775, Madison Square Station, New York City 10010, describes itself as being "published by the Alternative Press Syndicate, a nonprofit association of alternative newspapers and magazines." Following a number of articles on various aspects of alternative journalism it lists some 225 publications claimed as its membership. Among them are the following from the Seattle meeting: *Boston Phoenix; Creative Loafing; Hartford Advocate; New Haven Advocate; New Times Weekly,* Phoenix, Arizona; *The Real Paper,* Boston; *Valley Advocate,* Amherst, Massachusetts . . .

[14]The documentation of these statistics appears in the Appendix, but it is worth noting here that of the 50 largest U.S. cities, the four in which we found no underground/alternative press were Charlotte, Indianapolis, Omaha and El Paso.

Four Powerful Allies of the Alternative Press

[15]Richard Neville, *Play Power: Exploring the International Underground,* Vintage Books, N. Y., 1971, pp. 156-157.

[16]Robert Glessing, *The Underground Press in America,* Indiana University Press, Bloomington, Indiana, 1971, p. 14.

[17]For example, Allen Young, one of the founders of the underground press movement, and for three years a member of the staff of the revolutionary-extremist "Liberation News Service" wrote in the magazine *University Review* in November 1972 a lamentation about the falling away of the underground papers but saw a ray of hope "with added coverage of politics and the counterculture in *Rolling Stone,* the *Village Voice, Ms., More,* the hip FM stations and the book publishing industry."

An Alternative Roll Call

[18]*New Times* ceased publishing with its January 8, 1979 issue, an economic casualty.

[19]*Penthouse,* August 1974, p. 37.

[20]The editions of *New Times* from which the examples in this and the immediately preceding paragraphs were taken are, in the order of their mention, as follows: The headlines, Sept. 19, 1975; May 27, 1977; Apr. 15, 1977 and Sept. 30, 1977; President Kennedy drawing—April 18, 1975, and baby in flag diaper, Apr. 15, 1977; Abbie Hoffman story—May 30, 1975; Sam Lovejoy—Oct. 18, 1974; Hearst case story

quoted—Apr. 16, 1976; others were in Mar. 21, 1975 and Mar. 5, 1976.

[21]Robert Glessing, *The Underground Press in America*, Indiana University Press, Bloomington, Indiana, 1971, p. 16.

[22]*Ibid.*, p. 16.

[23]Henrik Hertzberg was listed on the *Win* masthead as far back as December, 1970, and as recently as June 30, 1977. He had a short, by-lined contribution in the May 1, 1975 *Win* in which he said he welcomed the communist victory in Vietnam not because it would produce a free society as we understand it, but as "a victory for something honorable in the human spirit." Syndicated columnist John D. Lofton, Jr., writing in the May 1978 *Conservative Digest*, scores Hertzberg for this article and another advocating U. S. unilateral disarmament in the August 1974 *Win*, indicating in his column that he had an exchange with Hertzberg over both articles.

Chapter Three

The Political Segment of the Alternative Press

[24]The shock of events at the Guyana commune of the "People's Temple" sent us back to the directories. *Alternative America* lists the "People's Temple" at its California headquarters as "Interracial, Spiritual, Community, Christian," on the basis of its alternative values. It is interesting to note Jones' patronage of alternative publications. Press reports indicate that in the litter scattered about his Jonestown home by looters were three publications considered in this study: the now defunct *Los Angeles Free Press*, the socialist *In These Times*, and the magazine *Seven Days*.

[25]Brian Crozier, *A Theory of Conflict*, Scribner's, New York, 1975, p. 81.

[26]Muller and Spahn, *From Radical Left to Extreme Right*, Campus Publishers, Ann Arbor, Michigan, 1970, p. 125.

[27]*Newsletter of the Democratic Left*, June 1976, p. 1.

[28]*Mother Jones*, July 1977, p. 29.

[29]*Ibid.*, p. 29.

[30]*Progressive*, June 1975, pp. 9-10.

[31]*Mother Jones*, July 1977, pp. 34 and 59.

Socialism

[32]*Socialist Revolution*, August 1972, p. 8.

[33]*In These Times*, promotional literature, 1972.

[34]*In These Times*, Vol. 1, No. 1, 1972, editorial page.

[35]*In These Times*, Nov. 16, 1977, p. 18.

[36]The *Militant*, Dec. 23, 1977, p. 24. The reference to "chapters of *In These Times* associates" denotes the paper's attempts to organize political affiliates around the country.

[37]The Dec. 6, 1978 edition of *In These Times* announced it had "become a

project of the Institute for Policy Studies."

[38]*In These Times*, Dec. 6, 1972, p. 15.

[39]Display advertisers, all taking full pages unless indicated otherwise by fractions, in order of appearance in the magazine were as follows: Harper & Row, book publishers; Quality Paperback Book Club; History Book Club; Save the Children, tax-exempt charity; Whole Food Company, New Orleans, ¼; *Christian Science Monitor*, newspaper; Warehouse Sound, hi-fi dealer; *National Lampoon*, magazine; California Cooperage, hot tubs dealer; *Marijuana Grower's Guide;* And/Or Books, Berkeley, ⅓; *New Times*, magazine; ASM Publishers, N.Y. ⅓; Tag Luggage, Santa Barbara, CA ⅓; *New Age*, magazine; and Newport cigarettes.

[40]*Mother Jones*, September 1978, page 5.

[41]For example, one used in 1977 came in a 6 × 9 envelope, the top portion of which was a portrait-quality photograph of a man's forehead overprinted in large orange type with, "IF YOU'VE GOT A HEADACHE . . . WE'VE GOT A CURE!" The bottom portion of the envelope is a bright orange with two "window" openings, one for the machine-produced address label and a circular one revealing a bright blue disc on which black print reads, "FREE!" Inside is a four-page letter set in open-spaced, easy-to-read type, and headlines in orange at the top: "WHAT HEADACHE, YOU SAY?" Then in the first two-line paragraph of the letter: "You name it. Politics. Energy. Sex. The environment. Want me to go on? Inflation. Sports. Business. The universities." At the end of the letter the reader is told "We think you'll be delighted with *Mother Jones*" and extended a "Special Introductory Rate . . . a 30% saving off the regular newsstand price . . . How about it? Willing to risk a postage stamp (that we pay for) just to see the brightest new magazine around? . . . P.S. Let me repeat . . . If at any time, you decide you want out—for any reason—we'll refund your subscription in full. Even on the last issue."
Next in the promotional mailer is a memo-sized slip of glossy paper, a bright green with large white headlines and easy-to-read black type, offering a free copy of a booklet entitled *The Big Ten*. This booklet is said to be "everything you need to know about the '70s" and teases: "Ever wondered which are the 10 worst papers in America? Or the 10 best cheap wines? Or the 10 biggest corporate polluters? Or the 10 dumbest politicians? Or the 10 best hiking trails? . . . It's only available through *Mother Jones*, and this $1.95 value is in limited supply."

[42]In a full page self-promotion ad, and under a ⅓ of the page headline reading "RAISE HELL WITH MOTHER JONES!" the magazine congratulated itself in this fashion:

"for its efforts, *Mother Jones* has
—sparked Ralph Nader to demand recall of 3 million cars that could immolate their occupants in an accident.
—kicked off a Congressional investigation into a defective nuclear power plant.
—sent one huge pharmaceutical company reeling with an exposé on its birth control device that can kill women who use it.
—been praised as 'the best slick radical publication in the country' (the *Boston Globe)*." *Mother Jones*, April 1978, p. 43.

[43]*New American Movement*, Nov. 1971, p. 10.

[44]*Ibid.*, p. 11.

[45]*Ibid.*, editorial page.

[46]*New York Times*, May 6, 1976, editorial page.

[47]Hearings before the Subcommittee on Internal Security of the Senate Com-

mittee on the Judiciary, March 17-18, 1976, published by U. S. Government Printing Office, Washington, D. C., 1976.

[48]*Newsworks*, April 11-17, 1976, p. 18.

[49]The spring and summer of 1976 seem to have been something of a transition period for obtaining information from inside establishment institutions. Radical political activists had always been alert for spontaneous "whistleblowers." They immediately rushed to the side of anyone who arose with a complaint or a report of wrongdoing inside government or business. The Naderites had been particularly attentive in this respect. Apparently, however, spontaneity had some serious drawbacks and there was an increasing tendency to try to "create" sources of inside information. Spontaneous blowing of the whistle came too slowly for the political militants, and it was unpredictable and uncontrollable. It might take years for someone inside a particular government agency, or a given corporation, to rise up with appropriate information. The radical wants to portray the system as being worse than it is, it is thus not unlikely, but actually impossible that *unassisted* dissatisfactions will satisfy him. In fact, it is just as likely that they might occur in the wrong places — even places embarrassing to his own efforts — but certainly not in the precise places he seeks them. Besides, self-motivated whistleblowers tend to be strong personalities, with their own ingrained value systems, concepts of integrity, and single-mindedness of purpose. They are often difficult to manage, and they may not bring along the desired information. At any event, there seems to have been an increased effort beginning in mid-1976 to *produce,* rather than wait for, whistleblowers. The PBC tapes to wives, and the $25,000 offers to secretaries, were simply indications of this trend, not the whole trend. Apparently, this is the type of thing the *New York Times* was laying at PBC's door, through — "the organizing of internal spy systems in family, business or community," its editors wrote. It was much more pervasive in the radical community than PBC. *Mother Jones* was in the process of making it a part of its "Hell Raising" with the corporations, and its parent organization, the Institute for Policy Studies, had been trying to institutionalize it in annual "Whistleblowers Conferences" beginning in 1977. In May of 1978 the American Civil Liberties Union and the New York University Law School co-sponsored the "First National Seminar on Individual Rights in the Corporation," with key addresses by prominent corporate executives, labor officials, and political figures — including Ralph Nader and Sen. Birch Bayh. There were some noble efforts by a few businessmen to uphold the view that their corporations were already sensitive to employee rights, but the main thrust of the meeting, attended by an audience of some 400 mostly liberal-leaning functionaries of labor, business, journalism and academia, was toward protecting the "rights" of the employee to "tell all" at his own discretion. Some participants even forecast legislation toward this end.

[50]This conference was reported by the July 17, 1978 *Washington Post* to be the fourth yearly gathering of the "children of the '60s . . . led and organized by some of the prominent young radical political activists of the 1960s . . . now scattered in government offices, community organizations and public interest groups from Washington, D.C. to Alaska." It is typical of the mixing and merging of underground, alternative and establishment activities.

[51]ACORN: *A*ssociation of (formerly Arkansas) *C*ommunity *O*rganizations for *R*eform *N*ow, a network of chapters of low-income families organized around such issues as labor, housing, tenancy, and consumer rights; begun in 1970 in Arkansas by a Massachusetts National Welfare Rights Organization branch chief, it subsequently spread to ten other states — Colorado, Florida, Iowa, Louisiana, Missouri, Nevada, Pennsylvania, South Dakota, Tennessee and Texas. Fair Share: similar network within Massachusetts. *Gay Sunshine:* homosexual magazine.

Great Speckled Bird: now-defunct Atlanta underground newspaper. The Midwest Academy: training school for activists and community organizers in Chicago, founded by former leaders of Students for a Democratic Society. Mobilization for Survival: organizational umbrella instigated by War Resisters League in an attempt to combine antinuclear-power movement with groups demanding unilateral U. S. disarmament. Red Cent Collective: Amherst, Massachusetts collective of socialist economics related to Boston-based publication *Dollars & Sense,* supplies articles to the alternative press attacking pro-free enterprise programs on campuses and in the media. US-China Peoples Friendship Association: network of local chapters nationwide, ostensibly organized to promote people-to-people communication, which receives school and library support but actually is a device designed and founded by American leftists to generate pressure on the U. S. government for pro-Peking-U. S. foreign policies. Youth Against War and Fascism: youth arm of Workers World Party, splintered from the Socialist Workers Party in 1950s because it considered SWP to be "too far right."

[52]*The Organizer's Manual,* Bantam Books, New York, 1971.

[53]*Washington Star,* November 5, 1972.

[54]Irwin Silber, *The Cultural Revolution: A Marxist Analysis,* Times Change Press, New York, 1970, pp. 31-32.

[55]*Barron's,* August 23, 1976.

[56]Paul Dickson, *Think Tanks,* Atheneum, New York, 1970, p. 278.

[57]Kirkpatrick Sale, *SDS,* Random House, N.Y., 1973, p. 288.

[58]*Village Voice,* February 21, 1977, p. 33.

[59]Paul Dickson, *Think Tanks,* Atheneum, New York, 1970, p. 280.

[60]*Ibid.,* p. 283.

[61]*Ibid.,* p. 284.

[62]*Ibid.,* p. 284.

[63]*Ibid.,* p. 286.

[64]*Ibid.,* p. 288.

[65]Richard Neville, *Play Power: Exploring the International Underground,* Vintage Books, N. Y., 1971, p. 11.

[66]J.B. Hutton, *The Subversives,* Arlington House, New Rochelle, N.Y., 1972.

[67]Walter Laqueur, *Terrorism,* Little, Brown & Co., Boston, Mass., 1977.

[68]*Barron's,* August 23, 1976.

[69]Paul Dickson, *Think Tanks,* Atheneum, N.Y., 1970, p. 276.

[70]Robert Glessing, *The Underground Press in America,* Indiana University Press, Bloomington, Indiana, 1971.

[71]Paul Dickson, *Think Tanks,* Atheneum, N.Y., 1970, p. 283.

[72]"Institute for Policy Studies," May 1977, Heritage Foundation, Washington, D. C.

The Alternatives Among Workers

[73]*In These Times,* Oct. 25-31, 1978.

The Overtly Marxist Alternatives

[74]*U.S. News & World Report,* Nov. 6, 1978, p. 64.

[75]*Radical America,* July-August 1972, p. 3.

[76]*Ibid.,* p. 9.

[77]*Ms.,* August 1972, p. 68.

[78]*Ms.* has never merely catered to the existing interests of women. It has always been persuasive, and political—a prime organ of "women's liberation." Now it is well-fed with advertising and not so brash but it, too, is "left of center and anti-Establishment." In its early editions it included a directory of "Women's Movement Publications," many of which were *undergrounds.* It had a "Where to Get Help" directory which included such old and traditionally far-left organizations as the National Lawyers Guild, Women Strike for Peace, and the Women's International League for Peace and Freedom. There were occasional allusions to guerrilla warfare, such as the above. And Marxism was openly discussed, or even put into comic strip format. For example, in the December 1972 edition of *Ms.* there was a four-page color strip in a series entitled "Mary Self-worth"—an obvious satire of "Mary Worth"—in which *Ms.*'s Mary counsels a girl student to date that "nice young Marxist" because he is interested only in her mind, instead of the school football hero who is only after sex.

[79]Eugene Methvin, *The Riot Makers,* Arlington House, New Rochelle, N. Y., 1970, p. 234.

[80]Recently a corporate head complained in a public address that inaccurate and unfair allegations made against his company by church groups had been instigated by NACLA. Also recently, several sources have insisted that one of the founders of NACLA was Rev. Brady Tyson, advisor on Latin America to former U. S. Ambassador to the U. N., Andrew Young. Staff and writer names are rare in later editions, but in Vol. 1, No. 2, March 1967, when the *NACLA Newsletter* was eight mimeographed pages, there was an article on NACLA's founding under the by-line of "Brady Tyson." He states the SDS was a "prime mover" in developing the organization and lists among the reasons: "We have been drawn together in the founding: Our common sense of dismay as we perceive the obstructionist role of the U.S. in Latin America" and "Our common commitment to the necessity of a far-reaching social revolution in Latin America." The publishing address of the *Newsletter* for that edition was "Room 924, 475 Riverside Drive, New York, New York 10027"—the building of the National Council of Churches.

Party Newspapers

[81]Kirkpatrick Sale, *SDS,* Random House, N.Y., 1973, p. 236.

[82]Kirkpatrick Sale, *SDS,* Random House, N.Y., 1973, p. 286.
Sale states that Tom Hayden, generally regarded as one of the founders of SDS, missed a crucial conference in which the organization's future was debated by opposing internal factions, because: " . . . The Communist Party's Herbert Aptheker [the party's chief theorist and Bettina's father] had invited him and Staughton Lynd, as representatives of the 'New Left' on a 'fact-finding' trip to

North Vietnam, the first American delegation to visit there." (p. 249)

[83]*Ibid.*, p. 286.

[84]Anthony Bouscaren and Daniel Lyons, *Left of Liberal,* Twin Circle, 1969, p. 228.

[85]*The Pink Sheet on the Left,* March 27, 1978, p. 3.

[86]*The Call,* Nov. 27, 1978, p. 1.

[87]From a Congressional report, "America's Maoist: The Revolutionary Union," U.S. House of Representatives, June 22, 1972, p. 40.

[88]*Ibid.*

[89]*Red Papers 1, 2, 3* (see footnote 90).

[90]FBI informant testimony is from "America's Maoist—The Revolutionary Union," House Internal Security Committee, U.S. Congress, 1972. *Red Papers 1, 2, 3* is a 70-page RCP (then called Revolutionary Union) booklet not dated but believed 1970. Other information on RCP and its members is from: FBI Annual Report, Dec. 1972; *SDS* by Kirkpatrick Sale, Random House, N.Y., 1973; *The Greatest Plot in History* by Ralph de Toledano, Arlington House, New Rochelle, N.Y., 1977; *1978 Yearbook on International Communist Affairs,* Hoover Institution, Stanford, Cal., 1978; *US-China Friendship Newsletter,* Nov. 1972, San Francisco; and *Guardian,* Feb. 9, 1972 and Dec. 27, 1972.

Chapter Four

Miscellaneous Support Services for Alternative Media

[91]Laurence Leamer, *The Paper Revolutionaries,* Simon & Schuster, New York, 1972, p. 86.

[92]Background on LNS was taken primarily from *SDS* by Kirkpatrick Sale, and *Paper Revolutionaries* by Laurence Leamer. The nature of LNS material was verified by direct examination of several packets. Subscriber and financial data came primarily from *Information Digest,* a privately operated newsletter published in Baltimore.

Alternatives to the Professions

[93]Bouscaren and Lyons, *Left of Liberal,* Twin Circle, 1969; Ralph de Toledano, *The Greatest Plot in History,* Arlington House, New Rochelle, N. Y., 1977; Petr Beckmann, *The Health Hazards of Not Going Nuclear,* The Golem Press, Boulder, Colo., 1976.

Religious Alternatives

[94]*Christianity and Crisis,* May 30 and June 13, 1977, p. 116.

[95]The *Other Side,* June 1978, p. 4.

[96]The *Other Side,* July 1978, pp. 11-12.

[97]*Sojourners,* January 1977, p. 38.

[98]*Sojourners,* May 1978, p. 14.

[99]*Lucha,* July-August 1977, p. 9.

[100]*Radical Religion,* Fall 1978.

The Sex Role in Alternative Media

[101]Jim and Andrea Fordham, *The Assault on the Sexes,* Arlington House, New Rochelle, N.Y., p. 112.

[102]*Ibid.,* p. 112.

[103]*Ibid.,* p. 113.

[104]*Ibid.,* p. 113.

[105]*Red Papers 1, 2 and 3.* Revolutionary Union, San Francisco, 1970, pp. 58-59.

[106]Jim and Andrea Fordham, *The Assault on the Sexes,* Arlington House, New Rochelle, N.Y., p. 117.

Some Concluding Observations

[107]Michael Novak, *The American Vision,* American Enterprise Institute for Public Policy Research, Washington, D. C., 1978.

APPENDIX

Selected List of Alternative Publications in the U.S.
(In print in 1978)

Names of publications, or the initials by which they are usually known, are in italics. Publishers are immediately beneath publication name. All of these publications are in a range of liberal to left. Thus, comments to that effect were not considered necessary in each case. The publication's area of interest is also frequently obvious from its title. Thus, comments were not made on those. The remark "APS member" means publication was listed by the Alternative Press Syndicate as one of its members.

ACAS
Association of
    Concerned African
    Scholars
Box 791
East Lansing, MI 48823

Access
1028 Connecticut
    Ave., NW
Washington, D.C. 20036

Monthly newsletter of
tips and information on
how activists may get
material into the
mass media.

ACORN News
Association of
    Community
    Organizations for
    Reform Now
523 West 15th Street
Little Rock, AR 72202

Newspaper of what was
originally *Arkansas
Community . . .* , a
radical organizing
operation coming out of
the "welfare rights"
movement. Now a
political force in 13
south/midwest states.

ACORN Newsletter
Midwest Energy
    Alternative Network

Governor's State
    University
Park Forest South,
    IL 60466

Bimonthly tabloid on
energy and
environment, related to
original *ACORN*.

Action for Children
Box 602
Los Angeles, CA 90026

Newsletter on public
child care.

*Action for Children's
    Television News*
Action for Children's
    Television, Inc.
46 Austin St.
Newtonville, MA 02160

Acts 4:32 Newsletter
1306 Hiawatha Lane
Comanche, IA 52730

On radical Bible study,
seeking to connect
Christianity with
collectivism.

Advocate
2121 South El Camino
    Real
San Mateo, CA 94403

Newspaper for
homosexuals. Could

easily be considered
pornographic.

AERO Sun-Times
Alternative Energy
    Resources
    Organization
435 Stapleton Bldg.
Billings, MT 59101

Monthly magazine,
Montana area, focuses
on "renewable sources
of energy," new
technology and "politics
of solar energy."

Africa News
Box 3851
Durham, NC 27702

Weekly paper that is
one of those at the heart
of movement in U.S. to
support African
"liberation" groups.

Africa Today
c/o Graduate School of
    International Studies
University of Denver
Denver, CO 80208

Quarterly. On the same
order as the above, but
has been in existence for
25 years.

Against the Wall
Box 444

Westfield, NJ 07091

Magazine, 10 issues yearly, claiming to deal with "self-liberation" and "voluntary alternatives." Counterculture.

Ain't I a Woman
Box 1169
Iowa City, IA 52240

Former *underground* paper, women's liberation and prolesbian.

Akwesasne Notes
Mohawk Nation
Via Rooseveltown, NY 13683

Five times yearly publication of the Indians of the Mohawk Nation, tabloid newspaper size, long a member of the underground/alternative press syndicate.

Alaska Advocate
Anchorage, AL 99501

All Together Journal
All Together
Suite 1416
205 W. Wacker Drive
Chicago, IL 60606

Counterculture.

Alternative America
Box 134
Harvard Square
Cambridge, MA 02138

Catalogue of 5,000 entries, alternative publications and organizations.

Alternative Currents
Alternative Energy
   Cooperative
San Francisco
   Ecology Center

13 Columbus Street
San Francisco, CA 94111

Newsletter published by nonprofit collective to promote "nonpolluting, renewable energy sources."

Alternative Media
Box 775
Madison Square Station
New York, NY 10010

Magazine published irregularly by what was formerly Underground Press Syndicate, includes list of members.

Alternatives
701 N. Eugene St.
Greensboro, NC 27401

Information on lifestyles and publications and organizations advocating "alternatives."

*Alternative Schools
   Network Newsletter*
2044 W. Grenshaw
Chicago, IL 60612

Published by loose federation of alternative schools. Lists schools.

Alternatives Journal
Box 33348
San Diego, CA 92103

Counterculture.

*Alternative Sources
   of Energy*
Rt. 2, Box 90A
Milaca, MN 56353

Bimonthly magazine.

*American Atheist
   Magazine*
Box 2117
Austin, TX 78768

Published monthly by

Dr. Madalyn Murray O'Hair.

Ann Arbor Sun
603 E. William St.
Ann Arbor, MI 48104

General coverage, radical politics.

Antipode
Box 225
West Side Station
Worcester, MA 01602

Marxist views on geography, development, planning, political economy.

Applesauce
National Alternative
   Schools Program
School of Education
University of
   Massachusetts
Amherst, MA 01003

Aquarian
1 The Crescent
Montclair, NJ 07042

Counterculture.

Arab Student Bulletin
Organization of Arab
   Students in the
   U.S. and Canada
Box 369
East Lansing, MI 48823

*Asianamerican
   Journey*
Agape Fellowship
322 S. Virgil Ave.
Los Angeles, CA 90020

Monthly tabloid, radical religious.

Atlanta Gazette
1189 Virginia Ave. NE
Atlanta, GA 30306

Attica News
219 East 10th St.
New York, NY 10003

Monthly publication of prisoners and other defendants in cases resulting from the Attica Prison riot of 1971. Far-left, pro-revolutionary involvement.

Austin Sun
404-B West 15th
Austin, TX 78701

Back Porch Radio
Box 466
Madison, WI 53701

Promotion of radical radio broadcasting.

Bard Observer
Box 83, Bard College
Annandale-on-Hudson, NY 12504

UPS/APS member.

Bay Area Worker
Box 40159
San Francisco, CA 94140

Berkeley Barb
Box 1247
Berkeley, CA 94701

Big Muddy Gazette
4407 Bassec Dr.
Tuscaloosa, AL 35401

General coverage, radical.

Big River News
Box 165
Mendocino, CA 95460

Underground/alternative press paper for years.

Black Panther
Black Panther Party
8501 E. 14th St.
Oakland, CA 94621

Black Scholar Magazine
Box 908
Sausalito, CA 94965

Monthly, strong advocate of "liberation" movements in Africa.

Black Star
Social Revolutionary
    Anarchist Federation
Box 92246
Milwaukee, WI 53202

Blue Sky
Box 1773
Boulder, CO 80302

Deals with cable TV and video in general.

Booklegger
555 29th Street
San Francisco, CA 94130

Quarterly published by and for library workers.

Borrowed Times
Box 1311
Missoula, MT 59801

UPS/APS member.

Boston Phoenix
100 Massachusetts Ave.
Boston, MA 02115

Both Sides Now
1232 Laura St.
Jacksonville, FL 32206

UPS/APS member.

Breakthrough
Prairie Fire Organizing
    Committee/John
    Brown Book Club
Box 40614, Station C
San Francisco, CA 94110

Extremely militant, far-left. Serves as "above-ground" support for terrorism in U. S., Europe and Mideast.

Briarpatch Review
330 Ellis St.

San Francisco, CA 94102

Quarterly on alternative economics, is communication medium of small network of "humanized businesses" called Briarpatch.

Broadside Press
12652 Livernoise
Detroit, MI 48238

Broken Barriers
Box 2369
New Orleans, LA 70176

Brother
Box 4387
Berkeley, CA 94704

Tabloid on "discrimination against" homosexuals.

Bugle American
Subdued Publications, Ltd.
("a staff-owned, nonprofit corporation")
Box 12486
Milwaukee, WI 53212

APS member.

*Bulletin of the
    Atomic Scientists*
1020-24 East 58th St.
Chicago, IL 60637

Has been deeply involved in antinuclear power movement.

*Bulletin of Conerned
    Asian Scholars*
Box W
Charlemont, MA 01339

Qtrly. popular with left activists.

*Business and
    Society Review*
Suite 31E
870 Seventh Ave.
New York, NY 10019

Says it "aims to root out corporate corruption."

CAGLA Newsletter
Chicago Area Group on Latin America
2546 N. Halstead St.
Chicago, IL 60614

CALA Newsletter
Community Action on Latin America/
Madison Campus Ministry
731 State St.
Madison, WI 53703

This and immediately preceding entry serve activism against "U.S. imperialism" in Latin America.

California Socialist
Room 213
3950 West 6th St.
Los Angeles, CA 90020

Call
Box 5597
Chicago, IL 60680

Weekly newspaper of the Communist Party (Marxist-Leninist). Very active in labor matters.

Campaigner
U.S. Labor Party/
National Caucus of Labor Committees
231 West 29th St.
New York, NY 10001

One of several publications of the highly militant and controversial far-left pseudoright network headed by Lyndon LaRouche/Lyn Marcus. See also *Executive Intelligence Review, Fusion,* and *New Solidarity.*

Canto Libre
Center for Cuban Studies
220 E. 23rd St.
New York, NY 10010

Bilingual qtrly. on art, music, folklore, and politics—pro-Cuban.

Capitol Hill News Service
968 National Press Bldg.
Washington, D.C. 20045

Nader news information service.

Carolina Quarterly
Box 1117
Chapel, Hill NC 27514

Catholic Agitator
605 N. Cummings St.
Los Angeles, CA 90033

Catholic Worker
36 E. First St.
New York, NY 10003

Founded by Dorothy Day and others in the 1930s, is for disarmament and against nuclear power. Fields teams of activists and organizers in labor and at protest actions.

Challenge
Progressive Labor Party
220 E. 23rd St.
New York, NY 10010

Chicago Reader
12 E. Grand Ave.
Chicago, IL 60611

Chicano Press Association
Box 31004
Los Angeles, CA 90031

China and US
U.S.-China Peoples Friendship Association

41 Union Square West,
Rm. 1228
New York, NY 10003

Far left and rather under the domination of the CP (ML). See the *Call* entry.

Christianity and Crisis
537 West 121st St.
New York, NY 10027

Citizen Intelligencer
Box 2262
Los Angeles, CA 90051

One of a number of anti-CIA, anti-FBI, assassination-conspiracy publications in the country.

City Star
156 Fifth Ave.
New York, NY 10010

Fitfully published splinter of the *Guardian.* Seeks to establish itself as a radical community weekly.

Civil Liberties Review
American Civil Liberties Union
22 East 40th St.
New York, NY 10016

Claridad
Toscania 1153
Urbanizacion Villa Capri
Rio Piodros, PR 00925

One of several publications taking a radical or revolutionary stance on Puerto Rico.

Coalition News
Coalition for the
  Medical Rights
  of Women
4079A 24th St.
San Francisco, CA 94114

Bimonthly that keeps
up with various
campaigns, such as
occupational health and
"sterilization abuse."

Co-Evolution Quarterly
Box 428
Sausalito, CA 94965

The *Whole Earth
Catalogue* in a new
format. Counterculture.

*Collector's Network
  News*
State Historical Society
816 State Street
Madison, WI 53706

A privately published,
irregularly appearing
booklet of news on the
status of
underground/alternative
publications.

College Press Service
1764 Gilpin St.
Denver, CO 80218

UPS/APS member.

Columbus Free Press
Box 3162
Columbus, OH 43201

UPS/APS member.

Come Unity
Box 15642
St. Petersburg, FL 33733

APS member.

Common Sense
2448A Mission St.
San Francisco, CA 94110

Weekly, socialist,
community newspaper.

Communities
Box 117
McMinnville, OR 97128

APS member.

*Community Service
  Newsletter*
Box 243
Yellow Spring, OH 45387

Bimonthly, on
community, land, and
economics.

*Computer Peace
  Interrupt*
291 Sterling Place
Brooklyn, NY 11238

Technology for
"computer people for
peace."

Conspiracy
National Lawyers Guild
558 Capp Street
San Francisco, CA 94110

Publication of
nationally organized
network of left-leaning
to far-left lawyers.

Consumer News
Consumer News, Inc.
813 National Press
  Bldg.
Washington, D.C. 20045

Corporate Action Guide
c/o Alternatives
1924 E. Third
Bloomington, IN 47401

Not a periodical, but a
manual for activism
against corporations.
Originated in
Washington, but now
available at
Bloomington address
for $3.90.

Corporate Examiner
Corporate Information
  Center

475 Riverside Drive,
  Room 566
New York, NY 10027

Publication produced
by activist group in the
National Council of
Churches building.
Concerned with policies
and practices of major
corporations with
regard to labor,
environment,
consumers, minorities,
etc.

Counterspy
Box 647, Ben Franklin
  Station
Washington, D.C. 20004

Sporadically published
magazine among those
specializing in attacking
the CIA, FBI, police
intelligence, business
information agencies,
etc.

Country Lady's Daybook
1211 Coleman Ave.
Felton, CA 95018

Counterculture.

Country Women
Box 51
Albion, CA 95410

Bimonthly on lifestyles
published by rural
lesbian community.

*Covert Action
  Information Bulletin*
Box 50257
F Street Station
Washington, D.C. 20004

The latest in the anti-
CIA publications by a
faction formerly part of
Counterspy above.
Instigated by CIA
defector Philip Agee,
and launched from the
Soviet-dominated
World Festival of

Youth in Havana in 1978.

Creative Loafing
Box 8006, Station F
Atlanta, GA 30306

Has begun and ceased publication several times. APS member.

*Crime and
  Social Justice*
Box 4373
Berkeley, CA 94704

Advertised as a "journal of radical criminology."

Critical Mass Journal
Citizens Movement for
  Safe and Efficient
  Energy
Box 1538
Washington, D.C. 20013

A Nader publication.

Cuba Review
Cuban Resource Center
Box 206
Cathedral Station
New York, NY 10025

Pro-Cuban. Claims to seek to promote communications between Americans and Cubans and to "counter U. S. and church policies which contribute to injustice in Cuba and Latin America." Qtrly., said by *Resources Catalogue* to be "funded by Protestant and Roman Catholic Church group."

Cultural Correspondence
c/o Dorrwar Bookstore
224 Thayer St.
Providence, RI 02906

Erratically published magazine on cultural history, usually selected or shaped to fit a leftist view.

Daily Brother
Box 217
Pine Grove Mills, PA
  16868

APS member.

Daily World
Communist Party of
  the United States
205 West 19th St.
New York, NY 10011

*D.C. Democratic
  Economics*
Strongforce
2121 Decatur Place,
  NW
Washington, D.C. 20008

Bimonthly, published by radical organization claiming to be promoting worker-community managed businesses.

D.C. Gazette
1739 Connecticut Ave.,
  NW
Washington, D.C. 20009

One of the oldest underground/alternative papers. Monthly, it covers local activist news and runs an annual catalogue of national alternative publications and organizations. APS member.

*Disarmament Action
  Guide*
Coalition for a New
  Foreign and Military
  Policy
120 Maryland Ave., NE
Washington, D.C. 20002

One of the pieces of material published by this coalition of 40 "religious, peace, labor, professional and social action" organizations. Designed for activism toward unilateral U.S. disarmament.

Dissent
509 Fifth Ave.
New York, NY 10017

Doing It
Urban Alternatives
  Center
Worthington, OH 43805

Bimonthly, devoted to "humanizing city life" through alternative economics, lifestyles, health care, etc.

Dollars & Sense
324 Somerville Ave.
Somerville, MA 02143

From its masthead: "We offer interpretations for current economic events from a socialist perspective to be of use to people working for progressive social change."

Door
Box 2022
San Diego, CA 92112

Drummer
4221 Germantown Ave.
Philadelphia, PA 19140

APS member.

Earthmind
5426 Boyer Rd.
Mariposa, CA 95338

Newsletter on alternative energy, especially wind power.

Earth News Service
24 California St.,
Suite 400
San Francisco, CA
94111

Alternative service to
radio and publications.

East West Journal
233 Harvard Street
Brookline, MA 02146

Monthly magazine
gives much attention to
"macrobiotic principle
of natural healing,
nutrition and
meditation and other
spiritual disciplines
from around the
world"—and to
environmental,
community and energy
issues.

Ecology Action
2225 El Camino Real
Palo Alto, CA 94306

*Ecology Center
Newsletter*
2179 Allston Way
Berkeley, CA 94704

Newsletter on "who's
doing what to the
environment, costs of
energy" and a bay area
ecology calendar.
Monthly.

Eco-News
Environmental Action
Coalition
235 East 49th St.
New York, NY 10017

Ten issues a year on the
environment for
children growing up in
cities.

Edcentric
The Center for
Educational Reform,
Inc.

Box 10085
Eugene, OR 97401

Qtrly., advocates
radical changes,
claiming present system
is characterized by
"discrimination and
dehumanization."

Elements
Transnational Institute
program of the
Institute for
Policy Studies
1901 Q St., NW
Washington, D.C. 20009

Monthly magazine
purporting to cover
worldwide issues of
"natural resources,
conservation and
alternative energy." Has
strong anticapitalist
flavor and focuses on
supporting "liberation"
movements in the
Middle East and Africa.

Environment
Scientists Institute for
Public Information
560 Trinity
St. Louis, MO 63130

Views workers and
consumers being taken
advantage of with
respect to the
environment.

Environmental Action
Environmental Action,
Inc.
1346 Connecticut Ave.,
NW
Washington, D.C. 20036

The Epworth Pulpit
Box 1561
Kansas City, MO 64132

Radical religious.

*Executive Intelligence
Review*

231 West 29th St.
New York, NY 10001

One of several U. S.
Labor Party
publications. See note
at *Campaigner.*

Express
Box 234
Merrick, NY 11566

APS member.

Fag Rag
Box 331
Kenmore Station
Boston, MA 02215

Homosexual
publication.

Family Synergy
Box 30103, Terminal
Annex
Los Angeles, CA 90030

Carries information on
various types of
"expanded families,"
and puts people in
touch with others of like
interests.

Features and News
6449 Benvenue
Oakland, CA 94618

Syndicate service for
alternatives.

Feminary
Whole Woman Press
Box 954
Chapel Hill, NC 27514

Nationally circulated
newsletter, feminist.

Feminist Art Journal
41 Montgomery Place
Brooklyn, NY 11215

Qtrly. articles on
women in the arts, both
past and present.

Feminist Press
Box 334

Old Westbury, NY 11568

Publishes biographies, reprints of women's writings from the past, children's books, and material for schools.

Feminist Studies
Women's Studies
    Program
University of Maryland
College Park, MD 20742

Fifth Estate
4403 Second
Detroit, MI 48201

Figaro
1070 Charles St.
New Orleans, LA 70130

First Issue
127 Main Street
Brattleboro, VT 05301

Fish Cheer
Box 1583
Pensacola, FL 32502

Tabloid of movement to organize fishermen along Gulf of Mexico.

Flame
Coalition on Women
    and Religion
4759 15th Ave.
Seattle, WA 98105

Newsletter, pro-ordination of women.

Folly
Box 1061
Bethlehem, PA 18018

APS member.

Food Co-op Nooz
106 Girard, SE, No. 110
Albuquerque, NM 87106

Bimonthly tabloid, disseminating tips and information to food cooperatives around the country.

FPS
2007 Washtenaw Ave.
Ann Arbor, MI 48104

Irregular newsletter attacking public schools—circulated the infamous "School-stoppers Textbook," of tips on how to disrupt classes. Part of the "Youth Liberation News Service." Member APS.

Free Flowing
108 1/2 Hayward
Ames, IA 50010

Primitive tabloid irregularly published by antinuclear movement in Iowa. One of a type of little papers circulated crudely across the country within antinuclear circles. Much of edition examined was copied either from the *Catholic Agitator* or *Win* magazine.

Free for All
Box 962
Madison, WI 53701

APS member.

Freeindeed
Box 261
Kutztown, PA 19530

Radical religious.

Free Palestine
Friends of
    Free Palestine
Box 21096,
    Kalorama Station
Washington, D.C. 20009

One of several pro-Palestinian papers.

Free Venice Beachhead
Box 504
Venice, CA 90291

APS member.

Friends of Micronesia
2325 McKinley Ave.
Berkeley, CA 94703

Newsletter advocating "liberation" in Micronesia.

Fusion
Fusion Energy
    Foundation/U.S.
    Labor Party
231 West 29th Street,
    13th Floor
New York, NY 10001

Another U. S. Labor Party publication, see note at *Campaigner.*

Fusion
909 Beacon St.
Boston, NA 02215

General alternative paper. No connection with *Fusion* immediately above.

Gala Review
Box 14142
San Francisco, CA
    94114

Homosexual/atheist/socialist publication.

Gar
Box 4793
Austin, TX 78765

APS member.

Gay Community News
22 Bromfield St.
Boston, MA 02108

Nationally circulated tabloid.

Gay Left
(published in England)
distributed in U.S. by
    Carrier Pigeon
88 Fisher Ave.
Boston, MA 02120

Gay News
(also published in
England—from 1A
Normand Gardens,
Greyhound Road,
London, W149SB)

Usually more than 30-
page tabloid, calling
itself "world's largest
circulation newspaper
for homosexuals,"
arrives in U.S. by mail
to subscribers and
libraries.

Gay Sunshine
Journal of Gay
  Liberation
Box 40397
San Francisco, CA 94140

Large in pages and
circulation.

Ghent Press
Box 1144
Norfolk, VA 23501

APS member.

Gotham City
Box 26, Village Station
New York, NY 10014

Gramma
(published in Cuba,
from Avenue General
Suarez y Territorial,
Plaza de la Revolucion
"Jose Marti," Apartado
6280, Havana, Cuba 70-
6521)

Well circulated in U.S.

Grapevine
Joint Strategy and
  Action Committee
National Council
  of Churches
475 Riverside Drive
New York, NY 10027

Radical activist, anti-
business.

Grass Roots

No. 1 Thomas Circle,
  Room 203
Washington, D.C. 20005

Greenhouse
Box 6091
Kansas City, MO 64110

APS member.

Green Mountain Films
Box 177
Montague, MA 01351

Collective which
arranges for production
and circulation of films
in support of
antinuclear movement.

*Green Mountain
  Quarterly*
462 North Main Street
Oshkosh, WI 54901

Claims to present
"outstanding analyses
on issues of social
urgency by
contemporary or
classical authors."

Green Revolution
3537 6th Ave.
San Diego, CA 92103

Ecology publication.

Gris Gris
121 North St.
Baton Rouge, LA 70130

Guardian
33 West 17th Street
New York, NY 10011

Probably the most
informative single
weekly source on
activities of the
American far left.

Guild Notes
National Lawyers Guild
853 Broadway,
  Room 1705
New York, NY 10003

Nationally circulated

bimonthly, of a network
of chapters heavily
peopled by far-leftists of
almost every stripe.

Gulf Solidarity
Gulf Solidarity
  Committee
Box 40155
San Francisco, CA 94140

Seeks to promote
support for "liberation"
forces in Arabian Sea
Gulf.

Haiti Report
Friends of Haiti
Box 348
New City, NY 10956

Promotes support for
"liberation" forces in
Haiti.

Hartford Advocate
495 1/2 Farmington Ave.
Hartford, CT 06105

APS member.

Headhunter
1210 Truxillo
Houston, TX 77004

APS member.

Health/PAC Bulletin
17 Murray Street
New York, NY 10007

Bimonthly, on health
issues from a leftist
political view.

Health Rights News
542 Dearborn St.
Chicago, IL 60605

High Times
Box 386 Cooper Station
New York, NY 10003

APS member.

Humanist
American Humanist
  Association/American
  Ethical Union

923 Kensington Ave.
Buffalo, NY 14215

Theoretical discussions of, and ideas for practical application of, humanism.

Iconoclast
Box 7013
Dallas, TX 75209

APS member.

Independent Eye
Box 19085
Cincinnati, OH 45219

APS member.

Indigena
Box 4073
Berkeley, CA 94704

One of several publications aimed at taking radical politics to American Indians.

Indochina Chronicle
Box 4000D
Berkeley, CA 94704

APS member.

Industrial Worker
Industrial Workers
  of the World
752 W. Webster St.
Chicago, IL 60614

APS member.

Inquiry
Cato Institute
1700 Montgomery St.
San Francisco, CA 94111

Monthly magazine that is a mixture of libertarian, conservative, and leftist materials. Inclusion of leftist articles seems to be the result of what are considered to be useful accommodations to such organizations as the Institute for Policy Studies.

Inside/Outside
Box 9083
Berkeley, CA 94709

Qtrly. newsletter on library services for youth and adults in prisons.

Insurgent
  Sociologist
Western Union of
  Radical Sociologists
c/o Department
  of Sociology
University of Oregon
Eugene, OR 97403

Qtrly. claiming to be "committed to the liberation of social science from bourgeois hegemony and to advancing contribution of social scientists to the transformation of capitalist society and building of socialism."

Integrity
701 Orange St., No. 6
Fort Valley, GA 31030

Homosexuals and religion.

Interchange
Breira
Box T, 200 Park Ave.,
  South, Rm. 1603
New York, NY

New Jewish publication, advertising in such media as *In These Times.*

Intercontinental Press
Box 116, Village
  Station
New York, NY 10014

Monthly magazine of Trotskyite views of world affairs.

Interface Journal
Box 970
Attica, NY 13503

Semiannual magazine on "alternatives for higher education."

Intermedia
2431 Echo Park Ave.
Los Angeles, CA 90026

Qtrly. that serves as a resource guide to performing groups, media of all kinds, and fund sources for "alternative" groups.

Internationalism
Box 961
New York, NY 10027

Intersection Newsletter
756 Union Street
San Francisco, CA 94133

Published by center for religion and arts.

In These Times
1509 North Milwaukee
  Ave.
Chicago, IL 60622

Weekly, should be a companion piece to *Guardian* for anyone wishing to keep up with the left in the U.S. This one reflects more closely those ideas and issues leftist lobbyists take to Capitol Hill. Now owned by the Institute for Policy Studies.

Iranian People's
  Struggle
Box 671
New York, NY 10026

Monthly newsletter, published by affiliate or revolutionaries in Iran.

*Issues in
Radical Therapy*
Box 23544
Oakland, CA 94623

Qtrly. published by collective of radical therapists.

*Journal of
Ecumenical Studies*
511 Humanities Bldg.
Temple University
Philadelphia, PA 19122

*Journal of
Homosexuality*
Haworth Press
149 Fifth Ave.
New York, NY 10010

*Journal of Sports
and Social Issues*
Institute for Sports and
Social Analysis
Virginia Wesleyan
College
Norfolk, VA 23502

*Journal of
World Education*
Association for
World Education
3 Harbor Hill Drive
Huntington, NY 11743

Promotes communications among institutions working toward a global view of education.

Jump Cut
Box 685
Berkeley, CA 94701

Six editions a year, radical criticism of current film in social and political sense.

Keep Strong
Intercommunal
Survival Committee
1222 West Wilson Ave.
Chicago, IL 60640

Monthly magazine, seeks political following among low-income tenants, the aged, and ethnic groups.

Know
Know, Inc.
Box 86031
Pittsburgh, PA 15221

Women's movement newsletter.

Koinonia Newsletter
Koinonia Partners
Rt. 2
Americus, GA 31709

Religious community, for years experimenting in communal ownership, often serves as host to radical groups such as antinuclear-power activists.

Korea Commentary
US-Korea Research and
Action Committee
Box 24175
Oakland, CA 94623

Bimonthly, news of "the left" in Korea.

Labor Newsletter
National Lawyers Guild
3276 East 14th Street
Oakland, CA 94601

See notation at *Guild Notes* for nature of NLG.

*Lancaster Independent
News*
23 Prince St.
Lancaster, PA 17604

APS member.

Lansing Star
Box 24
East Lansing, MI 48823

APS member.

Latin American

Film Project
Box 315
Franklin Lakes, NJ 07417

Films on Puerto Rico and Chile.

*Latin American
Perspectives*
Box 792
Riverside, CA 92502

Qtrly. theory for use in discussions of capitalism and socialism for teachers, students, and workers.

LAWG Letter
Latin American
Working Group
Box 22027
Station P
Toronto, Ontario
Canada M5S 2T2

Newsletter, bimonthly, well-circulated in the U.S.

Leftfield
Fight to Advance
the Nation's Sports
Box 19312
Washington, D.C. 20036

Monthly newsletter of Ralph Nader organization devoted to muckraking professional athletics.

Le'sbeinformed
Lesbian Resource
Center, Inc.
2104 Stevens Ave., South
Minneapolis, MN 55404

Lesbian Tide
8855 Cattaraugus Ave.
Los Angeles, CA 90034

Liberation
339 Lafayette St.
New York, NY 10012

Liberation News Service

17 West 17th St.
New York, NY 10011

Far-left "wire service" for alternative media.

Libertarian Connection
Box 90913
World Way Station
Los Angeles, CA 90009

Lincoln Gazette
545 South 29th St.
Lincoln, NE 68501

APS member.

Little Free Press
715 E. 14th St.
Minneapolis, MN 55404

Newsletter promoting "independence from heavy-consumption culture."

Los Angeles Free Press
5850 Hollywood Blvd.
Los Angeles, CA 90028

Los Desarraigados
Box 606
Notre Dame, IN 46556

Newsletter on Chicano workers and the church.

LSM News
Liberation Support
   Movement Press
Box 2077
Oakland, CA 94604

Qtrly. magazine, totally devoted to support of guerrilla organizations in other countries.

Lucha
Christians Concerned
   About Chile
136 S. Chapin St.
South Bend, IN 46625

Highly militant, small magazine, openly promoting the revolutionary left in Latin America.

*Mailing List of
   Movement
   Organizations*
3414 Spring Garden St.
Philadelphia, PA 19104

National catalogue of leftist groups.

Maine Times
41 Maine
Topsham, ME 04086

Majority Report
74 Grove St.
New York, NY 10014

Extremely militant women's lib.

Marijuana Monthly
Box 44428
Panorama City, CA 91402

APS member.

Marxist Perspectives
Cliomar Corp.
420 West End Ave.
New York, NY 10024

Match
Box 3488,
   College Station
Tucson, AZ 85722

APS member.

Maui Sun
900 Vineyard St.
Wailuku, HI 96793

MERIP Reports
Middle East Research
   and Information
   Project
Box 3122
Washington, D.C. 20010

Promotes "liberation" in Mideast.

Midnight Special
National Lawyers Guild
122 West 26th St.,
   Top Floor
New York, NY 10001

Aimed at inmates in prisons, and provided to them free. Bimonthly. See entry at *Guild Notes* for nature of NLG.

*Midwest Gay
   Academic Journal*
Gay Academic Union
   of Ann Arbor
3405 Michigan Union
Ann Arbor, MI 48109

Militant
14 Charles Lane
New York, NY 10014

Companion piece to *Guardian* and *In These Times* for those who want to keep abreast of left in the U. S., in this case, communism in the Trotskyite mold.

Mobilizer
Mobilization for
   Survival
1213 Race Street
Philadelphia, PA 19107

Monthly tabloid devoted entirely to the antinuclear movement in its most militant expression.

Monday
Victoria, British
Columbia, Canada

Monthly Review
62 West 14th St.
New York, NY 10011

Somewhat scholarly monthly roundup of anticapitalist and prorevolution material on many countries.

Mother Earth News
Box 70
Hendersonville, NC
28739

Ecology with
counterculture flavor.

Mother Jones
Foundation for National
Progress
607 Market St.
San Francisco, CA 94105

An Institute for Policy
Studies project.

Mountain Newsreal
Box 4146, University
Station
Tucson, AZ 85717

APS member.

Mountain Views
Box 148
Eureka Springs, AR
72632

Mount Nebo Flash
Rt. 1, Box 229
New Marshfield, OH
45766

APS member.

Moving On
New American
Movement
1634 N. Milwaukee Ave.
Chicago, IL 60647

*NACLA Report on
the Americas*
(formerly *NACLA's
Latin America &
Empire Report*, and
prior to that, the
NACLA Newsletter)
The North American
Congress on Latin
American is publisher
Box 57, Cathedral
Station
New York, NY 10025
or

464 19th Street
Oakland, CA 94612

One of the most
influential radical
operations against
traditional U.S. and
corporate activities in
Latin America.

*Native American
Solidarity Committee
Newsletter*
558 Capp Street
San Francisco, CA 94110

Aimed at American
Indians.

New Age
Box 4921
Manchester, NH 03108

*New American
Movement*
1634 N. Milwaukee Ave.
Chicago, IL 60647

New China Magazine
US-China Peoples
Friendship
Association
41 Union Square West,
Room 631
New York, NY 10003

Qtrly. that promotes
U. S.-China relations
unfailingly along
Peking lines.

New Citizen
1053 Gillespie St.
Schenectady, NY 12308

APS member.

New Dawn
Box 254
Mt. Morris, IL 61054

Slick-paper
counterculture
magazine for young
women.

New Frontier
Box 603

Laurel Springs, NJ 08021

APS member.

New Harbinger
North American
Student Co-op
Organization
Box 1301
Ann Arbor, MI 48106

Qtrly. claiming to
explore the "frontiers of
alternative economics."

New Haven Advocate
248 Park St.
New Haven, CT 06511

APS member.

*New International
Review*
Box 26020C
Tempe, AZ 85282

Qtrly. democratic
socialist.

New Patriot
The New Patriot
Alliance
343 South Dearborn,
Room 305
Chicago, IL 60605

Erratically issued
publication of group of
Marxists, humanists,
and labor radicals.

New Rochelle Bugle
740 Webster Ave.
New Rochelle, NY 10801

News & Letters
News and Letters
Committees
1900 E. Jefferson
Detroit, MI 48207

Ten issues yearly.
Twelve-year-old
newspaper of a political
action group professing
to be Marxist-
humanists, with
chapters in San

Francisco, Los Angeles as well as Detroit.

News & Review
1930 De La Vina St.
Santa Barbara, CA 93101

APS member.

*Newsletter of the
Democratic Left*
853 Broadway, Room 617
New York, NY 10003

New Socialist
Box 18026
Denver, CO 80218

New Solidarity
U.S. Labor Party
231 West 29th St.
New York, NY 10001

One of several U.S. Labor Party publications, see entry at *Campaigner.*

Newsworks
Box 21026
Washington, D.C. 20009

Defunct underground paper.

New Times
1 Park Ave.
New York, NY 10016

New Times
Box 721
Rock Island, IL

APS member.

New Times Weekly
Box 2510
Phoenix, AZ 85002

APS member.

*New Unionist
Newsletter*
Box 24155
Minneapolis, MN 55424

New Unity
Box 891

Springfield, MA 01101

APS member.

New World Review
156 Fifth Ave., No. 308
New York, NY 10010

Pro-Soviet communist publication.

North Carolina Anvil
Box 1148
Durham, NC 27701

APS member.

North Country Anvil
Box 37
Millville, MN

North Star
Box 661
Del Mar, CA 92104

Northwest Passage
Box 105
S. Bellingham, WA
   98225

APS member.

Nuclear Opponents
Box 285
Allendale, NJ 07401

APS member.

Nurses Signal
Gay Nurses Alliance
Box 5687
Philadelphia, PA 19123

Lesbian publication.

OB People's Rag
Box 7750
Ocean Beach, CA 92107

APS member.

Off Our Backs
1724 20th St., NW
Washington, D.C. 20009

Osawatomie
Box 2283
Seattle, WA 98122

Occasionally published communications support for Weather Underground, bomb-throwing splinter of SDS.

Other Side
The Other Side, Inc.
Box 12236
Philadelphia, PA 19144

Radical religious magazine.

Outlaw
1315 18th St.
San Francisco, CA 94107

Bimonthly, publication of the national Prisoners Union—inmates and ex-inmates.

Ozark Digest
Box 549
Eureka Spring, AR 72632

Pacific News Service
604 Mission Street,
   Rm 1001
San Francisco, CA 94105

Leftist wire service, producing pro-"liberation" movement material from countries scattered over the world.

Pacific Research
Pacific Studies Center
867 Dana Street,
   No. 204
Mountain View, CA
   94041

Six issues yearly, concerned with islands and countries in and around the Pacific.

Pacific Sun
Marin County, CA

Paper Rose
1810 SE 39th Ave.
Portland, OR 97214

Peoples World
1814 10th St.
Berkeley, CA 94710

People United
2515 Dwight Way
Berkeley, CA 94704

APS member.

Philadelphia Solidarity
GPO Box 13011
Philadelphia, PA 19101

Political Affairs
23 West 26th St.
New York, NY 10010

Communist Party
publication.

Portland Scribe
215 Southeast 9th Ave.
Portland, OR 97214

Weekly community
party and calendar of
counterculture and
radical activities.

Power Line
Environmental Action
   Foundation
74 Dupont Circle Bldg.
Washington, D.C. 20036

Newsletter,
consumerism toward
utility companies, and
antinuclear power.

Prairie Sun
(formerly *Sun Rise*)
Box 1483
Rock Island, IL 61201

*Praxis: A Journal of
   Radical Perspectives
   on the Arts*
Box 207
Goleta, CA 93017

Prime Time

420 West 4th St.
New York, NY 10036

"By and for older
women."

Primo Times
104 1/2 E. Kirkwood,
   No. 7
Bloomington, IN 47401

APS member.

Progressive
408 W. Gorham Street
Madison, WI 53703

Progressive Labor
Progressive Labor
   Party
GPO Box 808
Brooklyn, NY 11201

*Public Interest
   Economics*
1714 Massachusetts
   Ave., NW
Washington, D.C. 20036

Monthly. Theory,
cooperatives, antitrust,
energy, agriculture.

Public Interest Report
340 Chester-12th Bldg.
Cleveland, OH 44114

Newsletter of the "Ohio
Public Interest
campaign," a coalition
of church and
community
organizations advised
by the Institute for
Policy Studies,
combating industry
moving from state.

Public Occurrence
182 Main St.
Burlington, VT 05401

APS member.

Puerto Rico Libre!
Box 319 Cooper Station
New York, NY 10003

Monthly magazine
(pulp paper) of the P.R.
Solidarity Committee,
which seeks to promote
"national liberation" in
Puerto Rico.

Radical America
Box B
North Cambridge, MA
   02143
   or
60 Union Square
Somerville, MA 02143

Radical History Review
Mid-Atlantic Radical
   Historians
   Organization
Box 946
New York, NY 10025

Radical Religion
2401 Le Conte Ave.
Berkeley, CA 94709

Radical Teacher
316 W. 107th St.,
   Apt. 3A
New York, NY 10025

Qtrly., produced by the
Radical Caucus in
English and Modern
Language.

Radical Therapist
Box 1215
Minot, ND 58701

Rag
2330 Guadalupe
Austin, TX 78705

APS member.

Rama
1380 Howard
San Francisco, CA 94103

Razzberry
Box 24052
Dayton, OH 45414

Realist
Box 4027

San Francisco, CA 94101

Real Paper
929 Massachusetts Ave.
Cambridge, MA 02139

Recon
Box 14602
Philadelphia, PA 19134

Anti-U.S. Armed
Forces.

Resistance
Iranian Students
    Association in
    the U.S.
Box 4002
Berkeley, CA 94704

Resources
Box 134
Harvard Square
Cambridge, MA 02138

Resources Catalogue
Vocations for
    Social Change
5951 Canning Street
Oakland, CA 94609

One of catalogues used
in this study.

*Review of Radical
    Political Economics*
41 Union Square West,
    Room 901
New York, NY 10003

Revolution
Revolutionary
    Communist Party
Box 3486,
    Merchandise Mart
Chicago, IL 60654

Rising Up Angry
1215 W. Belmont
Chicago, IL 60614

APS member.

River City Review
Box 12725
Memphis, TN 38112

Rochester Patriot
277 N. Goodman St.
Rochester, NY 14607

APS member.

Rolling Stone
745 Fifth Ave.
New York, NY 10022

Root and Branch
Box 496
Cambridge, MA 02139

Rough Times
Box 89
West Somerville, MA
    02144

San Diego Reader
1100 Broadway
San Diego, CA 92101

*San Francisco
    Bay Guardian*
2700 19th St.
San Francisco, CA 94110

Sanity Now
Box 261
La Puente, CA 91747

APS member.

Science for the People
Scientists and
    Engineers for Social
    and Political Change
897 Main St.
Cambridge, MA 02139

Second City
1118 W. Armitage
Chicago, IL 60614

APS member.

Seditions
255 E. William
San Jose, CA 95112

Seven Days
206 Fifth Ave.
New York, NY 10010

Shelterforce
380 Main St.

East Orange, NJ 07018

Qtrly. for housing
activists and
community organizers.
APS member.

Signs of the Times
Old Chelsia
    Religious Education
Box 43
New York, NY 10011

Qtrly. "Journal for
Socialist Christians."

Simple Living
American Friends
    Service Committee
514 Bryant St.
Palo Alto, CA 94302

Extols lifestyles to
reduce consumption of
resources, by
organization that is in
the van of antinuclear,
procollectivist
movements.

Sipapu
Rt. 1, Box 216
Winters, CA 95694

For and by librarians.
APS member.

Sister
Box 597
Venice, CA 90291

Monthly tabloid,
militant feminist.

Sister
Box 467
North Hollywood, CA
    91603

Feminist.

Sister
250 Howard Ave.
New Haven, CT 06519

Monthly, feminist, legal
and health material.

Sisters
1005 Market St.,
Rm 402
San Francisco, CA 94101

Social Action
222 South Downey Ave.
Box 1986
Indianapolis, IN 46206

Bimonthly focusing on
"human rights," in
international relations.

Socialist Republic
League for Socialist
Reconstruction
Box 80, Madison
Sq. Station
New York, NY 10010

Socialist Review
4228 Telegraph Ave.
Oakland, CA 94609

Socialist Tribune
1012 N. 3rd St., RM 317
Milwaukee, WI 53203

Social Policy
184 Fifth Ave.,
Suite 500
New York, NY 10010

Five issues yearly,
leftist theory on
national issues.

*Social Questions
Bulletin*
Methodist Federation
for Social Action
Shalom House, 76
Clinton Ave.
Staten Island, NY 10301

Monthly, leaflet-size
publication of small but
national network of
militant and far-left
activists.

Sojourners
1029 Vermont Ave., NW
Washington, D.C. 20005

Monthly, religious

activist.

Southern Africa
156 Fifth Ave.
New York, NY 10010

Monthly, long-
established, nationally/
internationally
circulated pro-Marxist,
anti-U.S. presence in
Africa.

Southern Africa News
Box 29126
Washington, D.C. 20017

Bimonthly, similar to
the immediately
preceding.

Southern Exposure
Box 230
Chapel Hill, NC 27514

Southern Patriot
3210 West Broadway
Louisville, KY 40211

another at

411 Cowan St.
Nashville, TN 37208

APS member.

Spark
Box 1047
Detroit, MI 48231

Spartacist
Box 1377, GPO
New York, NY 10001

Weekly of the Marxist
Spartacist League.

Stamford Advocate
258 Atlantic St.
Stamford, CT 06901

Starship
Box 590
Stevens Point, WI 54481

APS member.

State and Mind
Box 89

Somerville, MA 02144

Straight Creek Journal
1521 15th St.
Denver, CO 80202

Strongforce
Strongforce, Inc.
2121 Decatur Pl.
Washington, D.C. 20008

Consumer, co-op
publication, advocates
"economic democracy."

Struggles
United Struggle Press
1133 Broadway
New York, NY 10010

Bimonthly, on "working
class movements" in
U.S. and other
countries.

Sun
Box 7217 North End
Detroit, MI 48202

APS member.

Survival Times
Community
Environmental
Council
109 E. De La Guerra
Santa Barbara, CA
93101

Swasia
Middle East and
Europe Working
Groups
Division of Overseas
Ministries
National Council
of Churches
475 Riverside Dr.,
Rm 626
New York, NY 10027

and

Box 29060
Washington, DC 20017

Weekly, focusing on
political struggles in

Southwest Asia and Africa, Persian Gulf.

Synergy
Box 4790
Grand Central Station
New York, NY 10017

Semiannual, directory of approximately 4,000 articles, books, plans, government reports, research groups, products lists, and facilities on solar energy, geothermal and other thermal energies, electrical energy, water and wind power, and energy storage.

Synthesis
Box 1858
San Pedro, CA 90733

Newsletter on citizen-worker self-management ideas and activities.

Take Over
Box 706
Madison, WI 53701

APS member.

Texas Monthly
Box 1569
Austin, TX 78767

Texas Observer
600 West 7th
Austin, TX 78701

Third World Newsreel
160 Fifth Ave.
New York, NY 10011

and related

California Newsreel
630 Natoma St.
San Francisco, CA 94103

Films promoting "liberation" forces in Africa and elsewhere in the developing

countries.

Tricontinental
Organization of Solidarity of the Peoples of Africa, Asia, and Latin America
POB 4224
Havana, Cuba

One issue a year, designed to promote Cuban views in U.S. and world on politics and economics in the Third World. Published in Spanish, English, and French.

Tricontinental Film Center
Box 4430
Berkeley, CA 94704

and

333 Avenue of the Americas
New York, NY 10014

Offer films showing leftist view of social, economic, and political situations.

Tricontinental News Service
30 East 20th St.
New York, NY 10003

Tulsa Free Press
2016 East 11st St.
Tulsa, OK 74101

APS member.

Twin Cities Reader
1801 University Ave.
Minneapolis, MN 55414

Union Wage
Box 462
Berkeley, CA 94701

Emphasis on working women.

United Ireland Newsletter
243 Mt. Hope Drive
Albany, NY 12202

Support for the IRA from U.S. sources.

Unity Struggle
Box 1181
Newark, NJ 07103

APS member.

University Review
2929 Broadway, NW
New York, NY 10027

USLA Justice Committee Newsletter
853 Broadway, Rm 414
New York, NY 10003

Weekly, deals with "political prisoner and human rights" matters.

Utopian Eyes
Box 1174
San Francisco, CA 94101

APS member.

Valley Advocate
57 Pratt, No. 808
Hartford, CT 06103

Valley Advocate
Box 851
Amherst, MA 01002

APS member.

Venceremos
Box 3169, GPO
New York, NY 10001

Monthly, by the organization that has arranged for American youth to go to Cuba for political indoctrination since the mid-1960s.

Village Voice
80 University Place
New York, NY 10003

WAIF 88.3 FM
2525 Victory Parkway
Cincinnati, OH 45206

Monthly program
guide and newsletter on
community radio.

Washington Monthly
1028 Connecticut Ave.,
  NW
Washington, DC 20036

Washington Watch
3308 Cedar
Lansing, MI 48910

Weather Report
Box 1221
San Marcos, TX 78666

The Weekly
Seattle, WA

Weekly People
914 Industrial Ave.
Palo Alto, CA 94303

White Lightning
Box 149, Jerome
  Ave. Sta.
Bronx, NY 10468

APS member.

Wild Currants
Box 11
Duluth, MN 55801

*Willamette Valley
  Observer*
454 Willamette St.
Eugene, OR 97401

APS member.

Win
503 Atlantic Ave.,
  Fifth Floor
Brooklyn, NY 11217

Another important
source of information on
activities of the militant
left in the U.S., along
with *Guardian* and *In
These Times*.

Witness
Box 359
Ambler, PA 19002

Woman Spirit
Box 263
Wolf Creek, OR 97497

Qtrly. poetry, fiction,
reviews of artwork,
lesbianism.

*Women: A Journal
  of Liberation*
3028 Greenmount Ave.
Baltimore, MD 21218

*Women's International
  Network News*
187 Grant St.
Lexington, MA 02173

Womens Press
Box 562
Eugene, OR 97401

Feminist newspaper.

*Women's Rights
  Law Reporter*
180 University Ave.
Newark, NJ 07102

Qtrly., covers
legislation and
information of legal
cases on women's
rights.

Worker
Box 3224
Seattle, WA 98114

Work Force
Vocations for Social
  Change
5951 Canning St.
Oakland, CA 94609

Connected with
Resources Catalogue.

Workers Power
14131 Woodward Ave.
Highland Park, MI 48203

APS member.

Workers Vanguard
260 West Broadway
New York, NY 10013

Workers World
46 West 21 Street
New York, NY 10010

*Working Papers for
  a New Society*
123 Mt. Auburn St.
Cambridge, MA 02138

WRL News
War Resisters League
339 Lafayette St.
New York, NY 10012

Parent organization of
Win, and active in the
antinuclear movement
internationally.

Zimbabwe News
Box 150
Glen Ellyn, IL 60137

Related to following.

*Zimbabwe News
  Bulletin*
Box 181
Bronx, NY 10453

Newsletter of the
ZANU Solidarity
Committee. Support for
"liberation" movement
in Africa.

INDEX
Publications

Extensive listings of alternative publications appear in the Appendix and on pages 20-22, 28-29, 47 and 67, and are not listed below.

INDEX
Groups and Individuals

The Rockford College Institute

The Rockford College Institute is devoted to the study of the cultural influences which shape the values and priorities of contemporary society. It endeavors to re-enlist the cultural forces in the advocacy of the ideals and principles which undergird liberty and capitalism. To this end the Institute publishes three regular periodicals:

> *The Rockford Papers.* Each issue provides several essays on a single theme. Recent issues have considered philosophical formulations and cultural phenomena that bear on the effectiveness of American politics and childhood education.

> *Chronicles of Culture.* (Bimonthly) Reviews and commentary about books, periodicals, movies and literary trends. The articles are written by scholars and critics committed to upholding the ideals and principles of the free society.

> *Persuasion At Work.* (Monthly) A newsletter that analyzes movements, groups and activities that bear favorably or unfavorably on the future of capitalism. Topics have included: the feminist movement, anticapitalist activism by church organizations, the marijuana mess, the Socialist Workers Party and anticapitalism in the regulatory bureaucracy.

On occasion, an essay of import is published separately, such as Leopold Tyrmand's *The Media Shangri-la,* which articulates the view that the press and electronic media manifest a growing tendency toward totalitarian attitudes, methodology and social practice.

In addition, the Rockford College Institute sponsors conferences on its own campus and provides seminars and lectures for national conventions, service clubs, corporate management meetings and various programs in other cities.

The research staff of the Institute not only monitors a wide range of influential publications that are not well-known, it also attends and reports on conventions of particular significance to the partisans of liberty and capitalism.

For details about memberships, subscriptions, back issues of publications, a copy of the annual report, or other information, contact:

Dr. John A. Howard, Director
Rockford College Institute
Rockford, Illinois 61101
Telephone: (815) 226-4016